1st Workshop on Language Technologies for Government and Public Administration (LT4Gov 2020)

AA007918

Marseille, France
11 – 16 May 2020

Editors:

Doaa Samy
David Perez-Fernandez
Jeronimo Arenas-Garcia

ISBN: 978-1-7138-1268-5

Printed from e-media with permission by:

Curran Associates, Inc.
57 Morehouse Lane
Red Hook, NY 12571

Some format issues inherent in the e-media version may also appear in this print version.

Copyright© (2020) by the Association for Computational Linguistics
All rights reserved.
Copyright for individual papers remains with the authors and are licensed under a Creative Commons 4.0 license, CC-BY-ND. (https://creativecommons.org/licenses/by-nd/4.0/)

Printed with permission by Curran Associates, Inc. (2020)

For permission requests, please contact the Association for Computational Linguistics at the address below.

Association for Computational Linguistics
209 N. Eighth Street
Stroudsburg, Pennsylvania 18360

Phone: 1-570-476-8006
Fax: 1-570-476-0860

acl@aclweb.org

Additional copies of this publication are available from:

Curran Associates, Inc.
57 Morehouse Lane
Red Hook, NY 12571 USA
Phone: 845-758-0400
Fax: 845-758-2633
Email: curran@proceedings.com
Web: www.proceedings.com

LREC 2020 Workshop
Language Resources and Evaluation Conference
11–16 May 2020

1st Workshop on Language Technologies for Government and Public Administration (LT4Gov)

PROCEEDINGS

Doaa Samy, David Pérez-Fernández and Jerónimo Arenas-García
(eds.)

Proceedings of the LREC 2020
1st Workshop on Language Technologies for Government and Public Administration
(LT4Gov)

Edited by: Doaa Samy, David Pérez-Fernández and Jerónimo Arenas-García

For more information:
European Language Resources Association (ELRA)
9, rue des Cordelières
75013 Paris
France
http://www.elra.info
Email: lrec@elda.org

© European Language Resources Association (ELRA)

These workshop proceedings are licensed under a Creative Commons
Attribution-NonCommercial 4.0 International License

Introduction

Welcome to the LREC2020 Workshop on "Language Technologies for Government and Public Administration (LT4Gov)" in its first edition.

LT4Gov stems from the experience gained by the organising team within the Spanish Plan for Advancement of Language Technologies. This Plan is a reference model of initiatives from the Governmental bodies to promote the introduction and integration of HLT in the workflow of different public entities.

LT4Gov is grounded on a strong believe that Human Language Technologies (HLT) could highly contribute in the innovation and the digital transformation of the public administration either in general or in domain-specific actions related to subsectors such as Education, Health, Culture, Tourism, etc. Thus, this workshop LT4Gov will invite contributions and results of work carried out by the HLT community in relation with public and governmental aspects in the line of language resources or in the line of solutions/tools destined either to these entities or to the citizen.

The sector of governmental bodies and public administration is an important sector representing a considerable percentage of expenditure of the GDP. Expenditure averages lie between 25%-57% in different countries according to reports from OECD, EU and World Bank. Moreover, this sector handles daily huge amounts of data in different formats.

Processing these huge amounts of information by HLT could provide valuable, data-driven and evidence-based insights that would highly impact the workflow for civil servants, the policy-making and the public services offered to citizens in different domains: Health, Tourism, Justice and Law, Culture.

LT4Gov aims at bringing together initiatives where Human Language Technologies (HLT) are used within the context of governmental bodies and public administration in the different domains (Health, Tourism, Justice, Culture, etc.). Governmental bodies and Public Administration Entities could be providers of data or could be users or beneficiaries of solutions in different sub-sectors. In addition, they could provide solutions to enhance services destined to the citizens.

Within LT4Gov and Public Administration, we consider the following three scenarios:

- PublicData4LRs (Public Data for Language Resources) - Public Administrations as providers of data
- LT4PolicyMaking (Language Technologies for Policy Making) - Public Administrations as users
- LT4Citizens (Language Technologies for Citizens) -Public Administrations as providers of services to the citizens

LT4Gov offer six use cases from different countries across the globe in which authors share their experience on how HLT was used in real scenarios within Public Administration and Governmental context. In its first edition, we hope LT4Gov would be a starting point to capture the attention of both the HLT community and the Public Administration on the benefits of applying LT in use cases that would impact the public services offered to citizens or would ease the daily work of civil servants. Finally, we hope researchers and stakeholders would gain useful insights and could find some inspiration in the presented use-cases.

On behalf of the Organising Committee,

Doaa Samy

Organizers:

Doaa Samy, Instituto de Ingeniería del Conocimiento (Spain) and Cairo University (Egypt)
David Pérez-Fernández, Plan de Tecnologías del Lenguaje, Secretaría de Estado para la Digitalización e Inteligencia Artificial (Spain)

Program Committee:

Jerónimo Arenas-García, Universidad Carlos III Madrid (Spain)
María José Del Olmo-Toribio, Secretaría de Estado para la Digitalización e Inteligencia Artificial (Spain)
David Griol-Barres, Universidad de Granada (Spain)
Maite Melero, Barcelona Supercomputing Centre (Spain)
Antonio Moreno-Sandoval, Universidad Autónoma de Madrid (Spain)
Pablo Haya-Col, Instituto de Ingeniería del Conocimiento (Spain)
Luis Fernando D' Haro, Universidad Politécnica de Madrid (Spain)

Table of Contents

Workshop Program

Proceedings of the First workshop on Language Technologies for Government and Public Admnistration (LT4Gov), pages 1–6
Language Resources and Evaluation Conference (LREC 2020), Marseille, 11–16 May 2020
© European Language Resources Association (ELRA), licensed under CC-BY-NC

Development of Natural Language Processing Tools to Support Determination of Federal Disability Benefits in the U.S.

Bart Desmet[1]* **Julia Porcino[1]*** **Ayah Zirikly[1]***
Denis Newman-Griffis[1,2] **Guy Divita[1]** **Elizabeth Rasch[1]**
[1]Rehabilitation Medicine Dept., Clinical Center, National Institutes of Health, Bethesda, MD
[2]Dept. of Computer Science and Engineering, The Ohio State University, Columbus, OH
{bart.desmet, julia.porcino, ayah.zirikly, denis.griffis, guy.divita, elizabeth.rasch}@nih.gov

Abstract

The disability benefits programs administered by the US Social Security Administration (SSA) receive between 2 and 3 million new applications each year. Adjudicators manually review hundreds of evidence pages per case to determine eligibility based on financial, medical, and functional criteria. Natural Language Processing (NLP) technology is uniquely suited to support this adjudication work and is a critical component of an ongoing inter-agency collaboration between SSA and the National Institutes of Health. This NLP work provides resources and models for document ranking, named entity recognition, and terminology extraction in order to automatically identify documents and reports pertinent to a case, and to allow adjudicators to search for and locate desired information quickly. In this paper, we describe our vision for how NLP can impact SSA's adjudication process, present the resources and models that have been developed, and discuss some of the benefits and challenges in working with large-scale government data, and its specific properties in the functional domain.

Keywords: disability, health, machine learning, NLP, information extraction

1. Introduction

The United States Social Security Administration (SSA) administers the largest federal programs for disability benefits in the US, serving over 15 million individuals (SSA Office of the Chief Actuary, 2019b; Social Security Administration, 2019). The SSA programs provide benefits to those individuals who are unable "to engage in any substantial gainful activity by reason of any medically determinable physical or mental impairment(s) which can be expected to result in death or which has lasted or can be expected to last for a continuous period of not less than 12 months" (Social Security Administration, 2012).

In order to determine whether an individual meets this definition of disability, SSA uses a five step process, illustrated in Figure 1. The first step is used to determine whether the individual meets the financial eligibility criteria. The second step looks at whether the applicant's alleged impairments are sufficiently severe. The third step evaluates whether the applicant meets certain medical criteria. If these criteria are met, the applicant will receive benefits. Otherwise, the case proceeds to the fourth and fifth steps, where SSA considers the individual's remaining functional capacity and the ability to work. Thus, both medical and functional information are critical to SSA's business process. To gather this information, adjudicators solicit medical records from the applicant's medical providers. This often results in hundreds or even thousands of pages of medical records for a single applicant, which the adjudicator must review manually to determine whether there is sufficient evidence to make a determination. This business process is further strained by the volume of applications – approximately 2 to 3 million new applications each year – and an aging work force where greater numbers of adjudicators

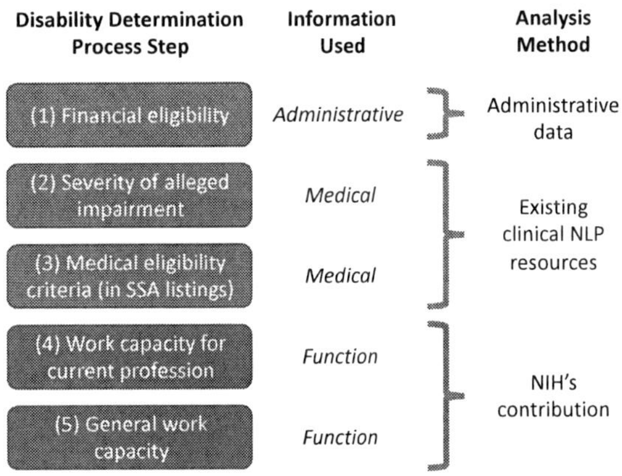

Figure 1: Illustration of the SSA disability determination process, indicating the primary type of information used at each step and relevant analytic methods.

will be retiring (SSA Office of the Chief Actuary, 2019a; United States Government Accountability Office, 2018).

In an effort to manage these challenges and better support adjudicators, the SSA has invested in developing natural language processing (NLP) systems for efficiently processing medical records. In addition, the SSA has recognized the importance of engaging external domain experts in order to introduce new perspectives and address key challenges. Through an inter-agency agreement with the National Institutes of Health (NIH), the two agencies have established a collaboration to develop novel NLP tools that particularly target information on function to help improve SSA's business process. This paper outlines the vision for these NLP tools at SSA, the current state of that vision, and what lessons have been learned.

*Equal contribution.

2. Vision for NLP in Disability Determination

The introduction of NLP into SSA's business process serves two critical goals: providing decision support and building a foundation for business intelligence. Decision support includes using NLP models to quickly identify information pertinent to a case, alerting adjudicators when documents contain relevant information, as well as providing tools that allow adjudicators to search for and locate desired information. Abbott et al. (2017) discussed the use of NLP to identify severely ill applicants to the Compassionate Allowance (CAL) initiative at SSA. On the other hand, business intelligence offers case support by checking for consistency of evidence when medical records are coming from different providers and covering months or even years of medical history. Developing systems for business intelligence also allows for a more global picture of data and business processes, such as by detecting fraud and making information more readily available for research purposes. The NIH-SSA collaboration has focused on decision support, where SSA's 5-step decision process offers an opportunity to combine the expertise of the two agencies.

Steps 2 and 3 of SSA's adjudication process are primarily concerned with medical information, such as documented symptoms, diseases, and disorders. A wide variety of NLP tools have been developed for identifying this information (Kreimeyer et al., 2017), and have proven useful even for identifying rare diseases (Udelsman et al., 2019). While there are known challenges in adapting medical NLP systems to language from the diversity healthcare providers interacting with a national consumer like SSA (Carrell et al., 2017), these tools nonetheless present significant potential to reduce adjudicator burden in reviewing medical evidence.

Steps 4 and 5, however, are concerned primarily with information on physical and mental function. Function, as conceptualized in the World Health Organization's International Classification of Functioning, Disability and Health (ICF), is determined not only by medical factors, but also by environmental and personal factors, and by the activities and social roles an individual chooses to engage in (World Health Organization, 2001). Anner et al. (2012) showed that the ICF framework is effective for evaluating disability. However, functioning information poses distinct problems for NLP, including inconsistent documentation standards, a lack of ontological and terminological resources capturing functional concepts, and a paucity of available data for NLP development and analysis (Newman-Griffis et al., 2019a). NIH's expertise in conceptualization and analysis of function thus offered a synergistic opportunity to focus on developing novel tools and resources to address these challenges in capturing functioning information with NLP.

The remainder of this paper describes NIH's initial research and development of NLP technologies for functional information.

3. Implementation

For initial research and development, NIH has focused on mobility reports, one of the most frequent areas of functional limitation involved in disability cases (Courtney-Long et al., 2015). Several types of NLP technologies have been developed for both document-level and case-level support, including information extraction and document ranking technologies, as well as the automated creation of terminologies supporting identification of functioning information.

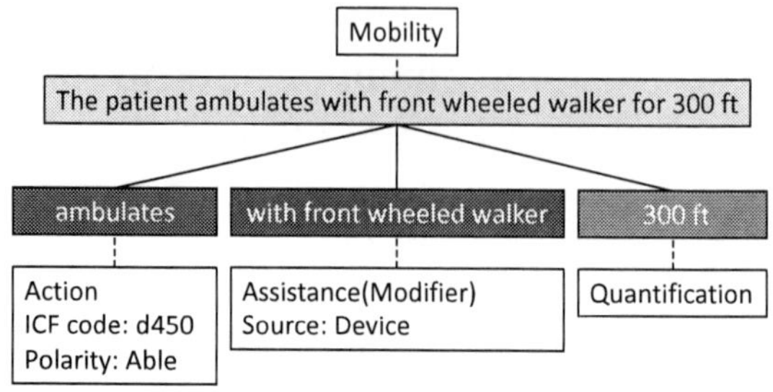

Figure 2: Annotation example of a Mobility report with subentities and attributes.

3.1. Data

Since functional information relevant to a claimant's allegations is primarily present in free text without structured codes associated with it, finding such information is a more time-consuming process for the adjudicators. In our developed models we focus on finding *activity reports* (Newman-Griffis et al., 2019a) that are relevant to a claimant's functional status. Examples of such information for mobility include `The patient is able to walk using a cane` and `The pt requires assistance to transfer from bed to chair.`

For the initial phases of research, we built our resources using data from NIH Clinical Center medical records as surrogate to SSA data. The NIH data are a rich source of information about function for terminology discovery and are often cleaner than SSA records.

A team of rehabilitation and medical experts developed schemas and guidelines for annotating mobility information. Spans of text related to a claimant's mobility status were marked in a corpus of 400 English-language physical therapy notes, provided by the Office of Biomedical Translational Research Information System (Cimino et al., 2014, BTRIS). Additional subentities and attributes were marked, as summarized in Figure 2.

Annotation results are presented in Table 1. Pairwise inter-annotator agreement as measured on a doubly-annotated set of 200 documents ranged from 96 to 98% F1 score on overlapping text spans (Thieu et al., 2017).

The resulting 400 annotated notes served as the gold standard for automatic Mobility report detection, and were randomly assigned to an 80/20 split into training and test sets.

3.2. NER Modeling

NIH introduced multiple information extraction baseline models that cast the problem as a named entity recognition (NER) task, where named entities are the functional information reports.

Type	Count	IAA (F1)
Mobility	4631	0.980
Action	4527	0.980
Assistance	2517	0.960
Quantification	2303	0.982
Score Definition	303	0.980

Table 1: Annotation results for the Mobility domain on 400 PT notes, and inter-annotator agreement on 200 doubly annotated PT notes.

As a baseline model, we used Conditional Random Fields (CRF) (Finkel et al., 2005) with an extensive list of features such as word shape, part-of-speech (POS) tags, word clusters, etc. Additionally, we test Bidirectional Long Short-Term Memory (BiLSTM-CRF) models, given their popularity and high performance in NER (Lample et al., 2016) and patient notes deidentification tasks (Dernoncourt et al., 2017). We tested both architectures to build mobility recognition models that handle the full mobility report span and its subentities. Both the CRF and Bi-LSTM-CRF models show promising results with respective token-level F1-scores of 82% and 78% for the mobility reports. Additionally, the models yield good results for subentities, with 75% and 83% token-level F1-score for *Action* mentions, which contain the most salient information for mobility-related queries.

These results are considerably lower than what NER systems typically achieve. For instance, state-of-the-art performance on the CoNLL 2003 dataset is 93.5% F1-score (Baevski et al., 2019). While this discrepancy can be partially attributed to the comparatively limited amount of training examples, we believe this is also caused by the challenging nature of the task, the large data variability and presence of noise (e.g. OCR). We refer to Newman-Griffis and Zirikly (2018) for further description and analysis of the results on a subset of the annotated reports.

To complement these modeling strategies, which yield high-precision predictions but suffer in recall, NIH also developed a recall-focused model that uses contextual information to estimate the likelihood that each token in a document is part of a mobility report (Newman-Griffis and Fosler-Lussier, 2019). This approach consistently identified over 90% of relevant tokens in NIH documents, though with an accompanying increase in false positives necessitating post review. Preliminary evaluation on SSA data has shown similar results; qualitative review of system outputs on diverse document types suggests effective generalization with only a small decrease in precision. These different strategies therefore offer useful alternatives for applications that may emphasize high-confidence predictions (e.g., document classification) or high-coverage (e.g., evidence retrieval).

3.3. Polarity Classification

Identifying relevant information is a key first step to help the adjudicators in their decision process. However, the next step in that process is providing the polarity of the functional report. For instance, given the mobility report in Figure 2, the polarity associated with the mobility action mention *ambulates* is *able*. The four polarity values in our annotation schema are *able*, *unable*, *unclear*, and *none*. Our proposed models range from rule-based systems, conventional machine learning techniques using random forests and support vector machines (SVM) to feed-forward (FF) and convolutional (CNN) neural network models. In addition we employ ensemble models that use majority voting between SVM and CNN, and a FF model that dynamically chooses output from the rule-based, SVM and CNN systems. Our proposed models predict the ability of a functional activity with 88% F1-score, as opposed to 69% for the *unable* label. This large gap in performance is mainly due to the imbalanced nature of the dataset. For further details about these models and analysis, we refer to Newman-Griffis et al. (2019b).

3.4. Document Ranking

Document-level information extraction technologies also offer an opportunity to support case-level processes, particularly document triage and prioritization. NIH has investigated using mobility reports extracted using NER models to rank a set of documents by the amount of predicted mobility information in each. These experiments yielded strong correlation with the true number of mobility reports in each document, indicating that NER technologies present significant utility for assisting case-level review of documents (Newman-Griffis and Fosler-Lussier, 2019).

3.5. Terminology Extraction

Terminologies and ontologies have been heavily developed and used for NLP in the clinical and biomedical domains. Examples of such repositories are the Unified Medical Language System (UMLS) (Bodenreider, 2004), the Systematized Nomenclature of Medicine Clinical Terms (SNOMED CT) (Donnelly, 2006) and the Human Phenotype Ontology (Robinson et al., 2008). SNOMED CT terminologies, for instance, provide over 90% coverage of the commonly used terms in medical problem lists (Elkin et al., 2006).

Given the utility of terminologies and the lack of any for the functioning domain, we developed them for multiple functioning domains including Mobility. A particular challenge for building these terminologies is that relevant terms in these domains are often not medical, but highly frequent and ambiguous. As a result, they need to be captured as multi-word units that include sufficient context (e.g. `able to walk around`), and the many different surface realizations of a concept needs to be generated to increase recall. We used neural models to expand seed terminology lists to achieve a partial-match coverage of 88% against annotated data.

4. Discussion

This project to develop models and tools for functional information to support SSA's business process has provided insight into the benefits and challenges of collaborations between federal agencies. At the same time, this is only a first step in the work to improve the decision-making process. In this section, we discuss some of the implications of collaborating across agencies, technical challenges, and future work aimed at addressing them.

4.1. Government Collaborations

The collaboration between SSA and NIH brings together expertise and knowledge across federal agencies to leverage process insights while providing new perspectives on ways to inform the disability determination process. There is a lot of work that goes into forming and maintaining such a relationship to ensure that the collaboration supports the mission of each agency and offers value to both. In particular, since SSA provides services to the American public, it is paramount that the collaboration protects the interests and privacy of those individuals who apply for benefits. In the US government, the Privacy Act protects information about individuals that is "retrieved by personal identifiers such as a name, social security number, or other identifying number or symbol" (Health and Human Services, 2019). SSA includes information about the Privacy Act as part of the disability benefits application, as well as any other form that collects information from an applicant (Social Security Administration, 1998). The Privacy Act prohibits the sharing of this information except if covered by one of twelve exceptions. These exceptions include use for research and statistical purposes, which therefore allows SSA to share these data with NIH as part of the collaborative effort to "enhance the decision-making process in the Social Security program" (Social Security Administration, 2020). While this exception allowed SSA to share these data, since the NIH is a research institute, we also sought the necessary human subjects' protection determinations for accessing and conducting research with the data. By leveraging the regulation processes across both agencies, we ensure that the necessary checks and balances are in place for protecting the data and the individuals the agencies serve.

4.2. Technical Challenges of SSA Data

While having access to these data is critical in order to develop systems that best suit SSA's business process, working with SSA records poses many challenges. SSA collects and generates enormous amounts of data for each applicant, and these data are often heterogeneous, noisy and fluid. Applicants' data include medical records from across the country and from all kinds of providers. Such a geographically diverse set of documents, with regional differences in use of language, and the evolution of language and medical jargon over time pose additional hurdles for developing NLP models.

Finding function information within this corpus inherently comes with challenges posed by the genre, where the terminology is under-specified and telegraphic at best, and text is often semi-structured. These properties exacerbate problems of scoping and ambiguity inherent in natural language, and make the genre resistant to traditional NLP techniques. Figure 3 illustrates these challenges with an example from the function domain. *Range of motion* (*ROM*), *within functional limits* (*WFL*) and *external rotation [strength]* (*ER*) are examples of telegraphic and ambiguous terminology. The example also contains two slot and value structures, for *ROM* and *Strength*. Strength observations are not enumerated (*all extremities*), and the shorthand *10/10 for all except* presents scoping issues, as it modifies the truth propositions from the previous statement. Improvements to any of these issues in the function domain are applicable more broadly. To that end, we are building systems to address scoping and decompose structured text using function as the use case.

ROM: All WFL for UE and LE's Strength: MMT was normal for all extremities. 10/10 for all except R sided GH ER 8/10

Body Function Type Body Location Qualifier

Figure 3: Example of terminological and structural ambiguity from the function domain.

5. Future Work

In ongoing work, we are developing classification models for other functional domains, tuning and validating them on SSA data, and supporting their integration at SSA.

5.1. From Demonstration to Deployment

Translating novel innovations in informatics research into operational practice in health systems faces a wide variety of challenges (Goldstein et al., 2004; Scott et al., 2018). A key challenge posed by current technologies lies in translating software designed for research and demonstration, which must be easily modifiable and typically focuses on small, controlled datasets, into products ready for enterprise-level deployment, demanding much greater robustness and the ability to process large-scale data rapidly. In NLP, two primary factors limit this translation: computational requirements and engineering environments. Cutting-edge technologies such as BERT (Devlin et al., 2019) require GPU capability for effective use, and present high demands for disk space and memory in processing and storing results; this imposes significant burden in procuring and maintaining sufficient computational resources to support the tools used. In addition, many current deep learning technologies use libraries implemented in the Python programming language, whereas Java is often the language of choice in secure government and enterprise environments, and for many medical NLP tools designed for large-scale use. Deployment might therefore necessitate reimplementation or interoperability layers.

6. Conclusion

Disability benefits case adjudication is an area of government functioning where human language technologies have the potential to improve service quality and cut costs. In an effort to address challenges with adjudicator case load, the US Social Security Administration is pursuing NLP solutions and reaching out to external partners with domain expertise that can help address the most challenging components. The SSA-NIH inter-agency agreement has been a success in bringing together experts from multiple domains, defining a modern vision and delivering tangible results that can improve SSA's business processes.

Acknowledgments

The authors would like to thank Pei-Shu Ho and Jonathan Camacho Maldonado for their annotation efforts. This research was supported in part by the Intramural Research Program of the National Institutes of Health, Clinical Research Center and through an Inter-Agency Agreement with the US Social Security Administration.

Bibliographical References

Abbott, K., Ho, Y.-Y., and Erickson, J. (2017). Automatic health record review to help prioritize gravely ill social security disability applicants. *Journal of the American Medical Informatics Association*, 24(4):709–716.

Anner, J., Schwegler, U., Kunz, R., Trezzini, B., and de Boer, W. (2012). Evaluation of work disability and the international classification of functioning, disability and health: what to expect and what not. *BMC Public Health*, 12(1):470.

Baevski, A., Edunov, S., Liu, Y., Zettlemoyer, L., and Auli, M. (2019). Cloze-driven pretraining of self-attention networks. *arXiv preprint arXiv:1903.07785*.

Bodenreider, O. (2004). The Unified Medical Language System (UMLS): integrating biomedical terminology. *Nucleic acids research*, 32(suppl_1):D267–D270.

Carrell, D. S., Schoen, R. E., Leffler, D. A., Morris, M., Rose, S., Baer, A., Crockett, S. D., Gourevitch, R. A., Dean, K. M., and Mehrotra, A. (2017). Challenges in adapting existing clinical natural language processing systems to multiple, diverse health care settings. *Journal of the American Medical Informatics Association*, 24(5):986–991, sep.

Cimino, J. J., Ayres, E. J., Remennik, L., Rath, S., Freedman, R., Beri, A., Chen, Y., and Huser, V. (2014). The National Institutes of Health's Biomedical Translational Research Information System (BTRIS): design, contents, functionality and experience to date. *Journal of Biomedical Informatics*, 52:11–27.

Courtney-Long, E. A., Carroll, D. D., Zhang, Q. C., Stevens, A. C., Griffin-Blake, S., Armour, B. S., and Campbell, V. A. (2015). Prevalence of disability and disability type among adults – United States, 2013. *MMWR. Morbidity and mortality weekly report*, 64(29):777–783, jul.

Dernoncourt, F., Lee, J. Y., and Szolovits, P. (2017). NeuroNER: an easy-to-use program for named-entity recognition based on neural networks. *arXiv preprint arXiv:1705.05487*.

Devlin, J., Chang, M.-W., Lee, K., and Toutanova, K. (2019). BERT: Pre-training of deep bidirectional transformers for language understanding. In *Proceedings of the 2019 Conference of the North American Chapter of the Association for Computational Linguistics: Human Language Technologies, Volume 1 (Long and Short Papers)*, pages 4171–4186, Minneapolis, Minnesota, June. Association for Computational Linguistics.

Donnelly, K. (2006). SNOMED-CT: The advanced terminology and coding system for eHealth. *Studies in health technology and informatics*, 121:279.

Elkin, P. L., Brown, S. H., Husser, C. S., Bauer, B. A., Wahner-Roedler, D., Rosenbloom, S. T., and Speroff, T. (2006). Evaluation of the content coverage of SNOMED CT: ability of SNOMED clinical terms to represent clinical problem lists. In *Mayo Clinic Proceedings*, volume 81, pages 741–748. Elsevier.

Finkel, J. R., Grenager, T., and Manning, C. (2005). Incorporating non-local information into information extraction systems by Gibbs sampling. In *Proceedings of the 43rd annual meeting of the Association for Computational Linguistics*, pages 363–370. Association for Computational Linguistics.

Goldstein, M. K., Coleman, R. W., Tu, S. W., Shankar, R. D., O'Connor, M. J., Musen, M. A., Martins, S. B., Lavori, P. W., Shlipak, M. G., Oddone, E., Advani, A. A., Gholami, P., and Hoffman, B. B. (2004). Translating research into practice: Organizational issues in implementing automated decision support for hypertension in three medical centers. *Journal of the American Medical Informatics Association*, 11(5):368–376, 09.

Health and Human Services. (2019). The Privacy Act. `https://www.hhs.gov/foia/privacy/index.html`.

Kreimeyer, K., Foster, M., Pandey, A., Arya, N., Halford, G., Jones, S. F., Forshee, R., Walderhaug, M., and Botsis, T. (2017). Natural language processing systems for capturing and standardizing unstructured clinical information: A systematic review. *Journal of Biomedical Informatics*, 73:14 – 29.

Lample, G., Ballesteros, M., Subramanian, S., Kawakami, K., and Dyer, C. (2016). Neural architectures for named entity recognition. *arXiv preprint arXiv:1603.01360*.

Newman-Griffis, D. and Fosler-Lussier, E. (2019). HARE: a flexible highlighting annotator for ranking and exploration. In *Proceedings of the 2019 Conference on Empirical Methods in Natural Language Processing and the 9th International Joint Conference on Natural Language Processing (EMNLP-IJCNLP): System Demonstrations*, pages 85–90, Hong Kong, China, November. Association for Computational Linguistics.

Newman-Griffis, D. and Zirikly, A. (2018). Embedding transfer for low-resource medical named entity recognition: A case study on patient mobility. In *Proceedings of the BioNLP 2018 workshop*, pages 1–11, Melbourne, Australia, July. Association for Computational Linguistics.

Newman-Griffis, D., Porcino, J., Zirikly, A., Thieu, T., Camacho Maldonado, J., Ho, P.-S., Ding, M., Chan, L., and Rasch, E. (2019a). Broadening horizons: the case for capturing function and the role of health informatics in its use. *BMC Public Health*, 19(1):1288.

Newman-Griffis, D., Zirikly, A., Divita, G., and Desmet, B. (2019b). Classifying the reported ability in clinical mobility descriptions. *arXiv preprint arXiv:1906.03348*.

Robinson, P. N., Köhler, S., Bauer, S., Seelow, D., Horn, D., and Mundlos, S. (2008). The human phenotype ontology: a tool for annotating and analyzing human hereditary disease. *The American Journal of Human Genetics*, 83(5):610–615.

Scott, P., Dunscombe, R., Evans, D., Mukherjee, M.,

and Wyatt, J. (2018). Learning health systems need to bridge the 'two cultures' of clinical informatics and data science. *Journal of innovation in health informatics*, 25(2):126–131, jun.

Social Security Administration. (1998). GN 03301.020 Privacy Act. https://secure.ssa.gov/apps10/poms.nsf/lnx/0203301020#b.

Social Security Administration. (2012). Disability Evaluation Under Social Security. https://www.ssa.gov/disability/professionals/bluebook/general-info.htm.

Social Security Administration. (2019). Annual report of the supplemental security income program. https://www.ssa.gov/oact/ssir/SSI19/ssi2019.pdf.

Social Security Administration. (2020). GN 03316.130 Disclosure Without Consent for Research and Statistical Purposes. https://secure.ssa.gov/apps10/poms.nsf/lnx/0203316130.

SSA Office of the Chief Actuary. (2019a). Disabled worker beneficiary statistics by calendar year, quarter, and month. https://www.ssa.gov/oact/STATS/dibStat.html (accessed: 02.12.2020).

SSA Office of the Chief Actuary. (2019b). Social Security Beneficiary Statistics. https://www.ssa.gov/oact/STATS/DIbenies.html (accessed: 02.12.2020).

Thieu, T., Camacho, J., Ho, P.-S., Porcino, J., Ding, M., Nelson, L., Rasch, E., Zhou, C., Chan, L., Brandt, D., et al. (2017). Inductive identification of functional status information and establishing a gold standard corpus: A case study on the mobility domain. In *2017 IEEE International Conference on Bioinformatics and Biomedicine (BIBM)*, pages 2319–2321. IEEE.

Udelsman, B., Chien, I., Ouchi, K., Brizzi, K., Tulsky, J. A., and Lindvall, C. (2019). Needle in a haystack: Natural language processing to identify serious illness. *Journal of Palliative Medicine*, 22(2):179–182. PMID: 30251922.

United States Government Accountability Office. (2018). Social Security Administration: Continuing leadership focus needed to modernize how SSA does business. https://www.gao.gov/products/gao-18-432t.

World Health Organization. (2001). *The International Classification of Functioning, Disability and Health: ICF*. World Health Organization, Geneva.

Proceedings of the First workshop on Language Technologies for Government and Public Admnistration (LT4Gov), pages 7–14
Language Resources and Evaluation Conference (LREC 2020), Marseille, 11–16 May 2020
© European Language Resources Association (ELRA), licensed under CC-BY-NC

FRAQUE: a FRAme-based QUEstion-answering system for the Public Administration domain

Martina Miliani*,†, Lucia C. Passaro†, Alessandro Lenci†
*Università per Stranieri di Siena, †CoLing Lab (Dipartimento di Filologia, Letteratura e Linguistica, Università di Pisa)
m.miliani@unistrasi.studenti.it, lucia.passaro@fileli.unipi.it, alessandro.lenci@unipi.it

Abstract

In this paper, we propose FRAQUE, a question answering system for factoid questions in the Public Administration domain. The system is based on semantic frames, here intended as collections of slots typed with their possible values. FRAQUE is a pattern-base system that queries unstructured data, such as documents, web pages, and social media posts. Our system can exploit the potential of different approaches: it extracts pattern elements from texts which are linguistically analysed by means of statistical methods. FRAQUE allows Italian users to query vast document repositories related to the domain of Public Administration. Given the statistical nature of most of its components such as word embeddings, the system allows for a flexible domain and language adaptation process. FRAQUE's goal is to associate questions with frames stored into a Knowledge Graph along with relevant document passages, which are returned as the answer. In order to guarantee the system usability, the implementation of FRAQUE is based on a user-centered design process, which allowed us to monitor the linguistic structures employed by users, as well as to find which terms were the most common in users' questions.

Keywords: Question Answering, Semantic Frames, Knowledge Graph

1. Introduction

Although late, Italy is slowly advancing in the digitization process of Public Administration data and services (Carloni, 2019). Now, more and more institutions in Italy manage data and delivery services on the web. Several municipalities started to adopt Question Answering Systems (QASs), chatbots, and digital assistants to ease citizens' access to public data. A wide range of citizens can use these systems since they permit to query vast repositories in natural language (Hovy et al., 2000; Ojokoh, 2018).

In this paper, we propose FRAQUE (FRAme-based QUEstion-answering), a domain-specific question answering system for factoid questions. Our system exploits semantic frames, here intended as templates consisting of a set of slots typed with their possible values (Minsky, 1974; Jurafsky and Martin, 2019). Thanks to frames, our QAS can query unstructured data, such as documents, web pages, and social media posts. We applied FRAQUE to the administrative domain in the Italian language. Nonetheless, the system is potentially adaptable to different domains and different languages. It relies on the statistical components of CoreNLP-it (Bondielli et al., 2018) for morphosyntactic analysis, which exploits the Universal Dependencies (UD) annotation scheme (Nivre, 2015). Statistical components are also employed for the semantic analysis of questions for Named Entity Recognition (NER) and term extraction. Finally, our system performs query expansion following an unsupervised approach based on word embeddings (Mikolov et al., 2013).

A first implementation of FRAQUE has been developed on the administrative domain. Our target users are municipality officers and common citizens who need to access the rich amount of information hidden in public documents. In particular, we decided to focus on citizens, who are supposed to use a QAS to get notice about municipality regulations and to receive other kind of information related to a certain administrative area. In order to guarantee the effectiveness and the usability of FRAQUE, we followed user-center design principles introduced by Gould and Lewis (1985).

We collected questions written by Italian native speakers to assess FRAQUE's outcomes. We tested FRAQUE on the administrative domain by employing the information extracted from a set of Italian documents including administrative acts, social media posts, and official municipality web pages. In particular, FRAQUE has been embedded into a dialogue management system and has been tested as a module of a larger project involving several instruments developed for the Public Administration (PA) domain.

The paper is structured as follows: An overview on QASs is given in Section 2., the definition of FRAQUE methodology is outlined in Section 3. The evaluation of the system in a real-case scenario is described in Section 4.

2. Related Work

Existing QASs have been categorized in different ways, e.g. depending on the addressed question type (e.g., confirmation questions, factoid questions, list questions), on the features of consulted data bases (e.g., full relational databases, RDF databases), on the adopted approaches and techniques (Ojokoh, 2018).

According to Dwivedi and Singh (2013) and Pundge et al. (2016) QASs can be distinguished into three different categories on the basis of the adopted approach: *linguistic approach* (Green et al., 1961; Clark et al., 1999; Fader and Etzioni, 2013; Berant et al., 2013), *statistical approach* (Moschitti, 2003; Ferrucci, 2010; Chen et al., 2017; Devlin et al., 2019) and *pattern matching approach* (Ravichandran and Hovy, 2002; Paşca, 2003).

QASs based on a linguistic approach exploit Natural Language Processing (NLP) and language resources such as knowledge-based or corpora. The knowledge architecture of these systems relies on production rules, logic, frames, templates, ontologies, and semantic networks (Dwivedi and Singh, 2013). On the one hand, the linguistic approach is very effective in specific domains. On the other hand, it shows limitations in portability through different domains, since building an appropriate knowledge base has usually heavy time costs. On the contrary, statistical approaches are easily adapted to various domains since they are independent of any language form. This kind of QASs are often based on Support Vector Machine (SVM) classifiers, Bayesian classifiers, Maximum Entropy models and Neural Networks (NN). Such question classifiers analyze the user's question to make predictions about the expected answer type, thanks to statistical measures. Statistical QASs require an adequate amount of data to train the models, therefore in this case the development cost moves from the manual production of linguistic rules to the preparation of annotated resources to feed the classifiers. Pattern matching approaches exploit text patterns to analyze the question to select and return the right answer. For example, the question "Where was Cricket World Cup 2012 held?" corresponds to the pattern "Where was `<Event Name>` held?" and is associated with the answer pattern "`<Event Name>` was held at `<Location>`" (Dwivedi and Singh, 2013). These systems are less complex than those exploiting linguistic features, which require time and specific human skills, and most of them automatically learn patterns from texts (Dwivedi and Singh, 2013; Hovy et al., 2000).

Furthermore, as reported by Jurafsky and Martin (2019), there are two different major paradigms of QASs: *information-retrieval based* and *knowledge-based.* In the former case, systems leverage on a vast quantity of textual information, which is retrieved and returned thanks to text analysis methods (Brill et al., 2002; Paşca, 2003; Lin, 2007; Fader and Etzioni, 2013; Chen et al., 2017; Devlin et al., 2019). In the latter case, semantic data are already structured into knowledge bases (Green et al., 1961; Clark et al., 1999; Ravichandran and Hovy, 2002; Fader and Etzioni, 2013; Berant et al., 2013). Finally, *hybrid systems*, like IBM Watson DeepQA (Ferrucci, 2010), rely both on text datasets and structured knowledge bases to answer questions.

Following such a classification, FRAQUE can be seen as an hybrid approach system. Firstly, it is based on linguistic analysis through statistical methods, which serves as prerequisite to maximize the performance of pattern matching techniques application. Secondly, it draws its data from a thesaurus and a Knowledge Graph (KG) both structured into semantic frames. In the thesaurus, simple terms, complex terms, and named entities related to the same frame are clustered and arranged into patterns exploited for the question analysis. In the KG, each slot frame contains a text passage (i.e., a single sentence *snippet*), selected through a ranking process measuring its relevance for that frame slot. Differently from relational databases, a pre-defined set of relations is not required by a KG, so that a more flexible object-oriented data storage is guaranteed (Miliani et al., 2019). Moreover, FRAQUE applies statistical techniques to identify and cluster data, such as word embeddings and classifiers.

3. The FRAQUE Methodology

In this section we present an overview of the user-centered design process employed to create FRAQUE. Moreover, we report on its components through the three main stages described in Dwivedi and Singh (2013), namely *document analysis*, *question analysis* and *answer analysis*.

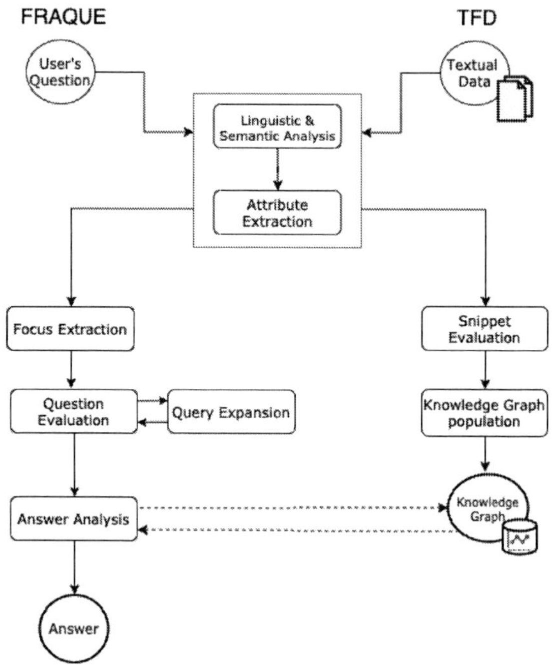

Figure 1: The diagram shows the FRAQUE analysis pipeline, which shares some modules with the Text Frame Detector (TFD) system (Miliani et al., 2019). Components in the central box belong to both FRAQUE and TFD systems. Except for the *answer analysis* component, all the other FRAQUE modules are employed in the *question analysis* described in Section 3.3.

3.1. User-Centered Design Process

We decided to adopt a user-centered design process (Gould and Lewis, 1985) to consider users' needs as a fundamental requirement for FRAQUE implementation. We distributed a questionnaire to 30 users divided into four age groups: $18-25$ (15%); $26-35$ (33.3%); $36-50$ (20%); $51-65$ (30%). We asked the users to write a small number of questions, pretending to interact with a QAS. The questionnaire allowed us to monitor the linguistic structures employed by users, as well as to find which terms were the most common in users' questions so that it was easier to identify frame triggers and attribute triggers. (see Section 3.2.). Further linguistic features detected by analyzing users' questions were: (i) lack of punctuation; (ii) variable length of questions: from 1 to 15 tokens (the shorter ones contained only keywords, as if the users were querying a search engine); (iii) typos. Considering (i) and (ii), we opted for avoiding fixed pattern for question analysis: we decided to look for patterns of unordered elements on the question text, without sticking to fixed term sequences.

3.2. Document Analysis

Document analysis consists of identifying candidate documents and detecting possible answers among document snippets (Dwivedi and Singh, 2013). The knowledge base employed by our system is a KG populated by the *Text Frame Detector* (TFD), an Information Extraction (IE) system described by Miliani et al. (2019) (see Figure 1), containing semantic frames selected through the design process described in Section 3.1. (see Figure 2).

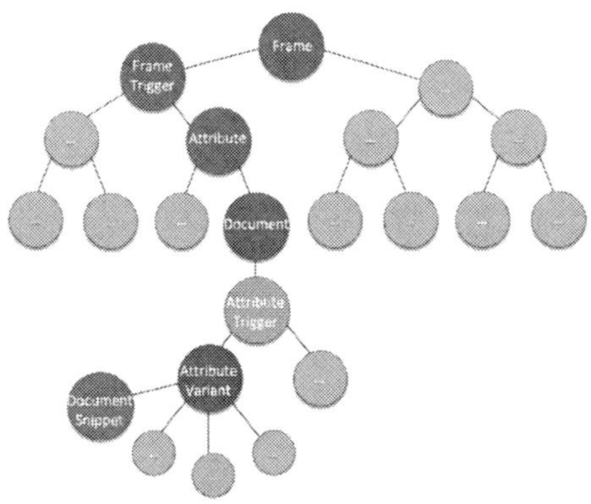

Figure 2: The Knowledge Graph structure employed by the TFD (Miliani et al., 2019).

3.2.1. Linguistic Analysis and preparatory IE process

As anticipated, FRAQUE and TFD have been embedded into a dialogue management system as the QAS of a chatbot. The systems are part of a bigger project that involves several instruments aimed at analyzing and indexing documents belonging to the PA domain. In particular, FRAQUE and TFD work downstream of a complex indexing process composed of both general purpose and domain specific components. First of all, TFD exploits two different linguistic pipelines: T2K^2 (Dell'Orletta et al., 2014) and CoreNLP-it (Bondielli et al., 2018). The former has been adapted for administrative acts analysis, the latter for the annotation of questions and texts like social media posts, since it includes statistical models for tokenization, sentence splitting, Part-of-Speech (PoS) tagging, and parsing. For event detection, our QAS exploits a model embedded in the broader system where it has been integrated. To extract NEs, the Stanford NER (Manning et al., 2014) is employed. In particular, it exploits the INFORMed PA (Passaro et al., 2017) model to extract entities related to the administrative domain. Furthermore, it employs EXTra (Passaro and Lenci, 2016) for in-domain complex terms extraction.

Table 1 shows the performances of the components used for the morphosyntactic and semantic analysis of texts. As anticipated, T2K^2 has been employed to analyze administrative acts, but to our knowledge its performances have not been assessed on the PA domain yet. We report an evaluation performed over general-purpose documents (Dell'Orletta, 2009).

Nevertheless, it is worth mentioning that morphosyntactic annotation underlying INFORMed PA, and EXTra was carried out with the adapted version of T2k^2 to the PA domain.

COMPONENT	PA	MEASURE	SCORE
T2K^2: PoS tagging	no	Accuracy	96.34%
CoreNLP-it: PoS tagging	no	F1	0.97
INFORMed PA	yes	$F1_{MacroAVG}$	0.77
EXTra	yes	Precision	93.50%

Table 1: Performances of each component exploited for the morphosyntactic and semantic analysis of texts in FRAQUE. The *PA* column indicates whether each module has been tested on the administrative domain.

3.2.2. Detecting Frames

In FRAQUE, each frame F encodes semantic categories relevant for a specific domain, such as the TAX frame for the administrative domain. "Municipality Tax" or "Garbage Tax" are linguistic cues called *frame triggers* (F_t) and enable the detection of frame instances on texts. **Deadline** and **methods of payment** are considered *attributes* (A). Attributes encode the relevant features of the semantic category represented by each frame. *Attribute triggers* (T) ease the attribute extraction from texts. T and Ft are both expressed by simple and complex terms, Named Entities (NEs), and Temporal Expressions (TEs). For instance, the **deadline** attribute is detected by the triggers "disbursement", "installment", and usually by date (see Figure 3). For ease of reading, the examples provided along the paper have been translated in English.

The [Municipality Tax]$_{tax}$ [disbursement]$_{payment}$ must be made through [wire transfer]$_{payment-form}$ or [postal order]$_{payment-form}$ in two [installments]$_{sum}$: [down payment]$_{sum}$ by [June 18th]$_{date}$ and [balance]$_{sum}$ by [December 17th]$_{date}$.

Figure 3: Example of a snippet expressing an instance of the TAX frame. It contains relevant information for both the **deadline** and the **methods of payment** attributes.

Triggers are stored in an thesaurus and linked to the related frames and attributes. They are registered with their standard form s and a small number of orthographic and morphosyntactic variants v selected by domain experts. Trigger variants are expanded with their semantic neighbors to improve frame and attribute recall. In Figure 3, the attribute triggers "wire transfer" and "postal order" are tagged with their standard form "payment-form".

After the linguistic analysis, we applied TFD to search frame and attribute triggers on the text, in the same or adjacent sentences. The snippet in Figure 3 shows the trigger for the TAX frame "Municipality Tax" along with several attribute triggers: simple terms, such as "disbursement" and "installment"; complex terms, like "wire transfer" and

"postal order"; and TEs, i.e. "June 18th" and "December 17th". The extracted sentences are ranked according to different scores, taking into account metrics like the number of retrieved triggers related to a given attribute, the average distance (in tokens) between the frame and the attribute triggers, the sentence length. Consider the snippet in Figure 3 concerning the attribute **methods of payment**: there are three retrieved triggers ("disbursement", "wire transfer" and "postal order"); the average token distance between the frame trigger "Municipality Tax" and these triggers is $(0+5+7)/3 = 4$ (e.g., "wire transfer" is five tokens distant from "Municipality Tax"); finally, the sentence length is 22 tokens.
The sentence with the highest rank is linked to the related attribute. More specifically, each candidate snippet receives a double score, a *Sentence Score* (SS), which ranks it within the set of snippets extracted from the same document, and a *Document Score* (DS) ranking it within the set of snippets extracted from the entire collection of documents (Miliani et al., 2019).
Frame instances are stored in a Neo4j[1] KG. As shown in Figure 2, each frame corresponds to a root node, which is represented by the TAX frame in the proposed example in Figure 4. Each *frame node* is connected with all the frame triggers found on the collection of documents. If we consider the snippet in Figure 3, the instance of the frame is given by the trigger "Municipality Tax", which labels the *frame trigger node* connected to "Tax" in Figure 4.
Frame trigger nodes are linked to attribute nodes. For instance, the snippet in Figure 3 contains information about the attribute **deadline**. This *attribute node* is connected to at least a *document node*, representing the document where the attribute has been extracted from: we took as example a "Rome Municipality Act". A snippet with the higher SS for the connected attribute is stored together with the document node. The snippet is also registered with its DS.
One of the triggers extracted from the snippet in Figure 3 is "June 18th", which labels the *trigger variant node*: this node is connected on one side to a *trigger node* marked by its standard form, i.e. "date", and on the other side to the *snippet node* representing the snippet containing the trigger.

3.3. Question Analysis

Question analysis includes parsing, question classification, and query reformulation (Dwivedi and Singh, 2013). The main goal of the question analysis module is to find a match between a question and at least a frame attribute indexed into the KG. The analysis is carried out exploiting some components shared with the TFD for the linguistic annotation and the frame extraction (See Fig. 1), a *focus detection* (Cooper and Ruger, 2000) and a *question evaluation* process, aiming at associating each question to the right frame and attribute and formulate the query to the KB. With the same goal, a *query expansion* module exploits word embeddings to find triggers among the semantic neighbours of questions ngrams (see Figure 1).

[1] http://neo4j.com/

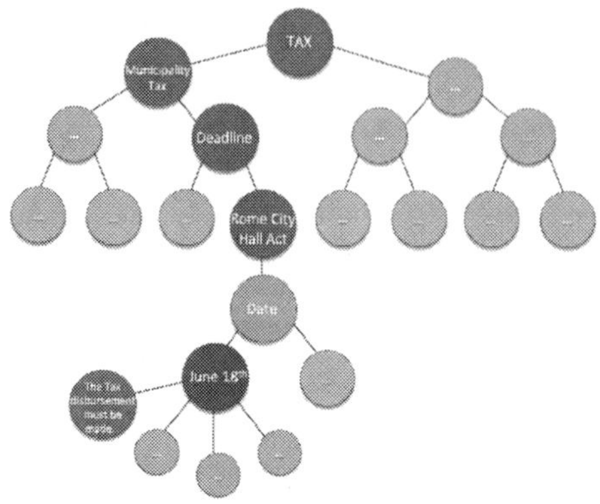

Figure 4: The Knowledge Graph populated by the TFD with an instance of the attribute **deadline**, belonging to the TAX frame.

The morphosyntactic analysis of questions is carried out by the CoreNLP-it pipeline, whereas rule-based components are exploited for NER. GATE[2] and the Stanford TokensRegex (Chang and Manning, 2014) are used to extract from questions the entities annotated with statistical components during the document analysis phase (See 3.2.1.).
Given a set of frame attributes A, an attribute $a \in A$ is identified in a question by the co-occurrence of a frame trigger F_t and a subset of the attribute triggers set T associated with it, such as $A = \{F_t, T\}$, where $T = \{t_1, ..., t_n\}$. Triggers are grouped by several standard forms $\{s_1, ..., s_n\}$, such as $S = \{s_1, ..., s_n\}$ (see Section 3.2.). Moreover, a subset Q of T is implicitly expressed on text by means of question foci. Thus, $Q \subset T$ and $S \subset T$.
The TFD module employed by FRAQUE for *attribute extraction* looks for a frame trigger F_t to possibly associate the question with a frame F. For instance, in this phase the frame trigger for the TAX frame "Municipality Tax" is extracted from the question in Figure 5. Then, the TFD searches for attribute triggers related to the TAX frame attributes. Different degrees of flexibility can be set for the attribute retrieving. A binary feature assigned to each trigger t_i suggests if the trigger is compulsory for associating an attribute with the examined question (Miliani et al., 2019).
In the example in Figure 5, the *attribute extraction* module detects only the generic trigger "payment", which led to associate the question with both the attributes **deadline** and **methods of payment**.

When the [payment]$_{payment}$ of the [Municipality Tax]$_{tax}$ is due?

Figure 5: Example of a user question containing the question focus ("when"). The tagged tokens are attribute triggers and tags correspond to their standard forms.

If no attribute is activated, a *query expansion* module checks if simple and complex terms extracted from questions are at least semantic neighbors of the triggers con-

[2] https://gate.ac.uk/

tained in the thesaurus. Semantic neighbors are computed within a distributional space trained with word2vec (Mikolov et al., 2013) on *La Repubblica* corpus (Baroni and Mazzoleni, 2004) and PaWaC (Passaro and Lenci, 2017) for administrative domain-specific knowledge. FRAQUE searches for the terms extracted from the question among the distributional space targets. Target words are lemmatized and combined for complex terms. Following the compositional property of word embeddings, each complex term vector consists of an element-wise sum of its word embedding elements (Hazem and Daille, 2018). Semantic neighbors are then detected among the terms with the highest cosine similarity measure. Among these neighbors, FRAQUE searches for triggers.

To solve the potential ambiguity resulting from the *attribute extraction* process and to facilitate a connection between questions and attributes, we implemented a *focus detection* module. The question focus is expressed by interrogative adverbs, like "how", and by equivalent linguistic expressions composed by more than one token, such as "in which way".

Each focus is associated with an attribute trigger. For instance "how" is linked to the trigger "methods", whereas the focus "where" is related to a trigger represented by a location named entity.

The extracted focus is then involved in the *question evaluation* process. In Figure 5, the question focus is "when", which is associated with TEs. Thus, the snippet containing the answer of the cited question must include a TE. The attribute including a date among its trigger is the attribute **deadline**, which is therefore associated with the question.

Can I $[\text{pay}]_{payment}$ the $[\text{Municipality Tax}]_{tax}$ with $[\text{postal order}]_{payment-form}$?

Figure 6: Example of a user question. The tagged tokens are attribute triggers and tags correspond to their standard forms.

If the focus extracted from the question is not connected to any frame attribute, or if no focus has been extracted from the question (as showed in Figure 6), a different procedure is followed. In this case, the attribute selected is the one with the highest *Attribute Score* (AS). The AS is computed for each candidate attribute selected by the *attribute extraction* module, and it is defined as:

$$AS = \frac{|S_Q|}{|S_T|} \times \frac{\sum_{i=1}^{n} cos}{|T_Q|} \tag{1}$$

where S_Q is the set of the standard forms of all the triggers T_Q extracted from the question and related to a certain attribute, such as $S_Q \subset S$ and $T_Q \subset T$. AS is directly proportional to the average of the cosine similarity between the triggers in T_Q and the triggers stored in the thesaurus. In this way, AS favors terms semantically closer to the triggers contained in the thesaurus, so that the noise resulting from query expansion process is reduced. Furthermore, AS does not consider only T_Q, the set of all triggers found on the question. AS takes into consideration the ratio between trigger standard forms in S_Q and T_Q, because it better expresses the variety of triggers by which an attribute is described on the text.

3.4. Answer Analysis

Finally, the extraction and ranking of candidate answers are carried out in the *answer analysis* (Dwivedi and Singh, 2013) (see Figure 1). The answer returned by FRAQUE is a snippet that is detected walking through the KG nodes, following a path indicated by the information extracted from the question during the *question analysis* phase. Once the question is analysed we identify three different scenarios:

- The *attribute* scenario: the question is associated with an attribute;
- The *frame* scenario: the question is linked to a frame, can be specified;
- The *residual* scenario: the question cannot be related to any attribute or frame.

In the first scenario, FRAQUE uses the question analysis results to query the KG and retrieve a snippet. Consider the question in Figure 5, which is related to the attribute **deadline** of the TAX frame, and which contains the frame trigger "Municipality Tax". FRAQUE looks at the root nodes inside the graph and selects the one labelled by "Tax". Then, it looks for "Municipality Tax" among the frame instances and checks for the presence of an *attribute node* tagged with "deadline" afterwards. At this point, if the requested information has to be extracted from the whole corpus, FRAQUE considers the snippets stored with each *document node* and returns the one with the highest DS. Otherwise, if the information has to be searched in a specific document (e.g., "Rome Municipality Act"), FRAQUE searches that document among those connected to the considered attribute, and returns the snippet associated with it.

In the *frame* scenario, only a frame trigger has been extracted from the question, but no focus or attribute trigger can disambiguate the user's information request. In this case, FRAQUE returns the document or the set of documents connected to the highest number of attribute nodes for the detected frame. Such documents are in fact supposed to contain a more complete knowledge about the frame itself.

In the *residual* scenario, triggers can not be detected neither among the question terms, nor among their semantic neighbours. In that case, FRAQUE extracts all metadata from the question, such as complex terms and entities, and uses them to query a document base indexed on Lucene[3]. In this database, the documents are indexed with terms, entities and topics related to the administrative domain. Terms and topics are structured in an ontology built by domain experts and employed for the platform SemplicePA (Miliani et al., 2017). FRAQUE returns those documents where the extracted terms and entities co-occur, by exploiting AND queries based on a list of pre-defined groups of metadata organized by type (i.e., terms, entities, and topic).

[3]https://lucene.apache.org/

4. Evaluation And Results

We evaluated FRAQUE on the administrative domain. In particular, we detected two frames: (i) the domain-specific TAX frame, and (ii) the EVENT frame, concerning the events taking place in a given city area, which we considered as a more general purpose frame (see Table 2). FRAQUE's outcomes are assessed on

To test our QAS, we selected 50 questions among those gathered through the questionnaire employed in the design process (see Section 3.1.), and among the FAQ reported on several Italian Municipality web sites. More precisely, we focused on a subset of questions referring to the target frames attribute (i.e., those asking information about events and taxes) and on another subset of questions not related to them. This way, we were able to evaluate the performances of the system for the three scenarios outlined in Section 3.4. Table 2 reports the frame attributes on which the performances of FRAQUE have been assessed.

FRAME	EVENT	TAX
ATTRIBUTES	Where When Cost	Deadline Methods of payment

Table 2: Attributes of the EVENT and TAX frames.

We evaluated FRAQUE on its ability to return (i) The right answer type; (ii) The right answer content. For what concern the first point, the goal is to assess whether the system is able to return the expected output type based on the scenarios described in Section 3.4. (i.e., *attribute*, *frame*, and *residual*). Traditional test accuracy metrics were employed, like F_1 *score*, which takes into consideration the overlap between the system outcomes and the correct answer type for each question.

	PRECISION	RECALL	F1-SCORE
macroAVG	0.69	0.57	0.61
microAVG	0.72	0.72	0.72

Table 3: Performances of FRAQUE for what concern the right answer type returned according to the detected scenario associated with the question.

Table 3 shows relatively low results for recall. Such a score is affected by the cases in which FRAQUE could not provide an answer to the question due to several reasons including (i) the absence of the information requested by the user and (ii) its ability to find the proper match within the question and the documents frames.

With regard to the second point (i.e., the answer content) a different evaluation was performed. A domain expert was asked to decide whether the returned snippets or documents (according to the detected scenario) contain the right answer to the questions. The metrics we used differ from one scenario to another (see Section 3.4.). Table 4 reports the FRAQUE's performances according to each scenario.

SCENARIO	MEASURE	PERFORMANCE
Attribute	MRR	0.58
Frame	MRR	0.75
Residual	Precision	0.59

Table 4: Evaluation of the content of the answers returned by FRAQUE according to the detected scenario. In the *frame* scenario, the system detected a frame, but no attribute related to it. In the *attribute* scenario, FRAQUE extracted at least a frame and an attribute from the text of the question. In the *residual* scenario, no frame could be extracted from the question text.

When the question can be associated with an attribute, as in the first scenario, we employed the *Mean Reciprocal Rank* (MRR). MRR is a metric introduced in the TREC Q/A track in 1999 for factoid question answering system evaluation (Jurafsky and Martin, 2019). For a set of questions N, it was computed on a short list of snippets containing possible answers, ranked by SS or DS (see Section 3.2.). Each question is then scored according to the reciprocal of the rank of the first correct answer. Given a set of questions Q:

$$MRR = \frac{1}{|Q|}\sum_{i=1}^{|Q|}\frac{1}{rank_i} \tag{2}$$

where $rank_i$ refers to the rank position of the first relevant document for the ith query. As for the *attribute scenario*, in table 5 we report a deeper evaluation over the various attributes.

FRAME	ATTRIBUTE	MRR
EVENT	Where	1
	When	0.75
	Cost	0
TAX	Deadline	0.60
	Methods of payment	0.50

Table 5: Evaluation of the answers to the questions related to EVENT and TAX frame attributes, according to the *attribute* scenario. The score is computed on the returned snippets.

It is important to notice that such results are highly affected by the **cost** attribute, for which the system was not able to find correct answers. Such errors are mainly due to a wrong indexed snippet for the corresponding attribute. Because of the high number of municipality acts stored in our database, most of the events have been extracted from this kind of documents. In most cases, these acts report how much the municipality spent to fund the events, instead of the ticket cost of the event. It is clear that we expect completely different results by evaluating the system on a knowledge base where information related to events is mainly extracted from social media posts, where the price of the ticket to participate in a certain event is usually specified.

In the *frame* scenario, the given question could not be associated with any attribute, so the documents containing relevant snippets for the detected frame are returned. Here, the MRR is calculated on the list of documents ranked by the number of the relevant snippets extracted from them and associated with the frame attributes. Table 6 shows the results for each frame concerning this scenario.

FRAME	MRR
EVENT	0.50
TAX	1
macroAVG	0.75

Table 6: Evaluation of the answers to questions related to EVENT and TAX frames, according to the *frame* scenario. The score is computed on the returned documents.

The low performance of the system in retrieving the information related to the EVENT frame is mainly caused by some features of the indexing process. TFD indexes a document only if it contains information relevant for at least one attribute. For this reason, even though the TFD stored an event in the graph, no document may be associated with it and thus returned.
In the *residual* scenario, no frame is associated to the question and the system queries a Lucene database with in-domain terms, entities, and topics extracted from the question text. In this case, FRAQUE returns up to 5 documents. Since the results are not ranked, the system performance was evaluated considering if at least one of the returned documents was actually relevant for the question. The employed evaluation metric is a variant of the precision: we considered as *true positive* only those cases where FRAQUE returned at least a relevant document for each query (seeTable 4). We decided to consider this metric also taking into consideration the QAS usage context, where the real goal is to guarantee that the information the user needs is among the returned documents.
The results showed that, in some cases, the queries returned no answers. On the one hand, this happens because we decided to maximize the quality of the returned results by employing AND queries in querying the Lucene database. Specifically, output documents were required to contain all (or pre-defined groups) of the relevant metadata identified in the text of the question. However, this way, the system never retrieves documents containing different combinations of terms, entities or topics extracted from the question. On the other hand, the errors are caused by the absence of documents related to the question topic. By evaluating FRAQUE without considering questions for which the Lucene database does not contain the needed information, the precision increases by 29%, reaching overall a performance of $0,76$.

5. Conclusions

In this paper we introduced FRAQUE, a question answering system based on semantic frames. FRAQUE structures textual data into frames so that they can be queried by means of natural language. This solution is based on an IE module for *document analysis*, namely the TFD (Miliani et al., 2019), allowing for the indexing of documents by text frames. Given this kind of metadata, FRAQUE is able to detect correct answers contained into document snippets and to associate them to frame attributes stored in a KG. FRAQUE has been integrated into a Dialogue Management System (DMS) as the question answering component of a chatbot, designed to give information about Italian Public Administrations.
However, in-domain linguistic analysis and resources in FRAQUE are easily portable to other domains, thanks to its statistical components, such as word embeddings, adopted in the query expansion module.
We evaluated FRAQUE in several real case scenarios obtaining encouraging results. The results calculated over the frames annotated with the TFD module reach an average MRR of $0,667$, whereas FRAQUE reaches a $0,59$ precision score in those questions not answered exploiting frames. Of course, there is still room for improvement, but if we consider only the cases where TFD performs well, FRAQUE reaches even higher results. By looking at these outcomes, we are led to believe that improving the TFD performances, the FRAQUE's ones can be drastically improved as well.
In the near future we plan to compare the obtained results with those of available related systems, at least on the first of the scenarios detected, where document snippets are returned as answer. Moreover, further development of our work will focus on the conversion of FRAQUE thesaurus to open standards, such as the *Resource Description Framework* (RDF), with the consequent adaptation of FRAQUE modules to this data model. This could ease the application of FRAQUE on existing resources, as well as facilitate other frameworks to exploit FRAQUE in-domain thesaurus.

6. Acknowledgements

This research has been supported by the Project "SEM il Chattadino" (SEM), funded by Regione Toscana (POR CreO Fesr 2014-2020). Besides the CoLing Lab, project partners include the companies ETI3 s.r.l. (coordinator), BNova s.r.l. and Rigel Engineering s.r.l.

7. Bibliographical References

Berant, J., Chou, Andrew Frostig, R., and Liang, P. (2013). Semantic parsing on freebase from question-answer pairs. In *Proceedings of the 2013 Conference on Empirical methods in natural language processing (EMLNP)*.

Bondielli, Passaro, and Lenci. (2018). CoreNLP-it: A UD pipeline for Italian based on Stanford CoreNLP. In *CliC-it 2018*.

Brill, E., Dumais, S., and Banko, M. (2002). An analysis of the askmsr question-answering system. In *Proceedings of conference on Empirical methods in natural language processing (EMLNP)*. Association for Computational Linguistics.

Carloni, E. (2019). Algoritmi su carta. politiche di digitalizzazione e trasformazione digitale delle amministrazioni. *Diritto pubblico*, 25(2):363–392.

Chang, A. X. and Manning, C. D. (2014). Tokensregex: Defining cascaded regular expressions over tokens. *Stanford University Computer Science Technical Reports. CSTR*, 2:2014.

Chen, D., Fisch, A., Weston, J., and Bordes, A. (2017). Reading wikipedia to answer open-domain questions. In *ACL*.

Clark, P., Thompson, J., and Porter, B. (1999). A knowledge-based approach to question-answering. In *Proceedings of AAAI*, pages 43–51.

Cooper, R. J. and Ruger, S. M. (2000). A simple question answering system. In *Text REtrieval Conference (TREC)*.

Dell'Orletta, F., Venturi, G., Cimino, A., and Montemagni, S. (2014). T2kˆ 2: a system for automatically extracting and organizing knowledge from texts. In *Proceedings of the Ninth International Conference on Language Resources and Evaluation (LREC-2014)*, pages 2062–2070.

Dell'Orletta, F. (2009). Ensemble system for part-of-speech tagging. *Proceedings of EVALITA*, 9:1–8.

Devlin, J., Chang, M.-W., Lee, K., and Toutanova, K. (2019). Bert: Pre-training of deep bidirectional transformers for language understanding. In *NAACL HLT*, pages 4171–4186.

Dwivedi, S. K. and Singh, V. (2013). Research and reviews in question answering system. *Procedia Technology*, 1(10):417–424.

Fader, Anthony, Z. L. and Etzioni, O. (2013). Paraphrase-driven learning for open question answering. In *Proceedings of the 51st Annual Meeting of the Association for Computational Linguistics*. Association for Computational Linguistics.

Ferrucci, D. (2010). Build watson: an overview of deepqa for the jeopardy! challenge. In *Proceedings of 19th International Conference on Parallel Architectures and Compilation Techniques (PACT)*. IEEE.

Gould, J. D. and Lewis, C. (1985). Designing for usability: key principles and what designers think. *Communications of the ACM*, 25(3):300–311.

Green, B. F. J., Wolf, A. K., Chomsky, C., and Laughery, K. (1961). Baseball: an automatic question-answerer. In *Awestern joint IRE-AIEE-ACM computer conference*. ACM.

Hazem, A. and Daille, B. (2018). Word embedding approach for synonym extraction of multi-word terms. In *Proceedings of the Eleventh International Conference on Language Resources and Evaluation (LREC 2018)*, Miyazaki, Japan, May. European Language Resources Association (ELRA).

Hovy, E., Gerber, L., Hermjakob, U., Junk, M., , and Lin, C.-Y. (2000). Question answering in webclopedia. In *Text REtrieval Conference (TREC)*.

Jurafsky, D. and Martin, J. H. (2019). Speech and language processing. Third edition draft on webpage: `https://web.stanford.edu/~jurafsky/slp3/`. Accessed: 3 July 2019.

Lin, J. (2007). An exploration of the principles underlying redundancy-based factoid question answering. *ACM Transactions on Information Systems (TOIS)*, 25(2):6.

Manning, C., Surdeanu, M., Bauer, J., Finkel, J., Bethard, S., and McClosky, D. (2014). The stanford corenlp natural language processing toolkit. In *Proceedings of 52nd annual meeting of the association for computational linguistics: system demonstrations*, pages 55–60.

Mikolov, T., Sutskever, I., Chen, K., Corrado, G. S., and Dean, J. (2013). Distributed representations of words and phrases and their compositionality. In *Proceedings of NIPS 2013, 26th Conference on Advances in Neural Information Processing Systems*, pages 171–178, Lake Tahoe, Nevada, USA.

Miliani, M., Passaro, L., Gabbolini, A., Passaro, L., Leci, A., and Battistelli, R. (2017). Semplicepa: Semantic instruments for public administrators and citizen. In *GARR*.

Miliani, M., Passaro, L. C., and Lenci, A. (2019). Text frame detector: Slot filling based on domain knowledge bases. In *Proceedings CliC-it 2019, 6th Italian Conference of Computational Linguistics*, Bari.

Minsky, M. (1974). *A framework for representing knowledge*. Massachusetts Institute of Technology, Cambridge, MA.

Moschitti, A. (2003). Answer filtering via text categorization in question answering systems. In *Proceedings of 15th IEEE International Conference on Tools with Artificial Intelligence*. IEEE.

Nivre, J. e. a. (2015). Universal dependencies 1.2. LINDAT/CLARIN digital library at the Institute of Formal and Applied Linguistics (ÚFAL), Faculty of Mathematics and Physics, Charles University.

Ojokoh, Bolanle ans Adebisi, E. (2018). A review of question answering systems. *Journal of Web Engineering*, 17(8):717–758.

Passaro, L. C. and Lenci, A. (2016). Extracting terms with Extra. *Computerised and Corpus-based Approaches to Phraseology: Monolingual and Multilingual Perspectives*, pages 188–196.

Passaro, L. C., Lenci, A., and Gabbolini, A. (2017). Informed pa: A ner for the italian public administration domain. In *Fourth Italian Conference on Computational Linguistics CLiC-it*, pages 246–251.

Paşca, M. (2003). *Open-Domain Question Answering from Large Text Collections*. CSLI.

Pundge, A. M., Khillare, S. A., and Namrata Mahender, C. (2016). Question answering system, approaches and techniques: A review. *International Journal of Computer Applications*, 141(3):0975–8887.

Ravichandran, D. and Hovy, E. (2002). Learning surface text patterns for a question answering system. In *Association for Computational Linguistics conference (ACL)*. Association for Computational Linguistics.

8. Language Resource References

Baroni, M., Bernardini, S., Comastri, F., Piccioni, L., Volpi, A., Aston, G. and Mazzoleni, M. (2004). *La Repubblica*.

Passaro, Lucia C. and A. Lenci. (2017). *PaWaC - Public Administration Web As Corpus*.

Proceedings of the First workshop on Language Technologies for Government and Public Admnistration (LT4Gov), pages 15–21
Language Resources and Evaluation Conference (LREC 2020), Marseille, 11–16 May 2020
© European Language Resources Association (ELRA), licensed under CC-BY-NC

Enhancing Job Searches in Mexico City with Language Technologies

Gerardo Sierra[1] **Gemma Bel-Enguix**[1] **Helena Gómez-Adorno**[1]
Juan-Manuel Torres-Moreno[2,3] **Tonatiuh Hernández-García**[1] **Julio V. Guadarrama-Olvera**[1,4]
Jesús-Germán Ortiz-Barajas[1] **Angela María Rojas**[4] **Tomas Damerau**[4]
Soledad Aragón Martínez[4]

[1]Universidad Nacional Autónoma de México, México, [2]LIA-Université d'Avignon, France,
[3]Polytechnique Montréal, Canada, [4]Secretaría del Trabajo y Fomento al Empleo (STyFE), México
{gsierram, gbele, thernandezg, jortizb}@iingen.unam.mx, helena.gomez@iimas.unam.mx,
juan-manuel.torres@univ-avignon.fr, {jvicente.go, angela.styfe} @gmail.com, {tdamerau, haragonm}@cdmx.gob.mx

Abstract

In this paper, we show the enhancing of the Demanded Skills Diagnosis (DiCoDe: Diagnóstico de Competencias Demandadas), a system developed by Mexico City's Ministry of Labor and Employment Promotion (STyFE: Secretaría de Trabajo y Fomento del Empleo de la Ciudad de México) that seeks to reduce information asymmetries between job seekers and employers. The project uses webscraping techniques to retrieve job vacancies posted on private job portals on a daily basis and with the purpose of informing training and individual case management policies as well as labor market monitoring. For this purpose, a collaboration project between STyFE and the Language Engineering Group (GIL: Grupo de Ingeniería Lingüística) was established in order to enhance DiCoDe by applying NLP models and semantic analysis. By this collaboration, DiCoDe's job vacancies system's macro-structure and its geographic referencing at the city hall (municipality) level were improved. More specifically, dictionaries were created to identify demanded competencies, skills and abilities (CSA) and algorithms were developed for dynamic classifying of vacancies and identifying terms for searches on free text, in order to improve the results and processing time of queries.

Keywords: Language Technologies for Citizens, Job Search, Information Retrieval

1. Introduction: Context of the job search in Mexico City

Mexico City (CDMX) has about 9 million inhabitants and it is the most populous federative state and city in the country with 5,967 inhabitants per square kilometer density (INEGI, 2020). In the fourth quarter of 2019, there were 4.5 million economically active inhabitants, of which 230 thousand are unemployed. Among the latter, about a third of them are young people (15-24 years old) and 38 percent young adults (25-44 y.o.), implying that the majority of the unemployed are young job seekers in full productive age (STyFE, 2019). Beyond unemployment, high and pervasive informality work rates intensify labor market (LM) inefficiencies and reduce decent job opportunities. Informal employment is defined as all paid work that is not regulated or protected by legal frameworks (OIT, 2020). One of the main problems between LM demand (LMD, which are employers) and LM supply (LMS, which are job seekers) is information asymmetry that affects job search effectiveness (Hart, 1983). Identifying the job profiles and skills required by LMD and comparing them with those brought along by LMS is one of the key goals of this project. This requires great efforts in systematizing a variety of data sources (CVs, job vacancies, training programs' contents, etc), among which the focus, so far, has been on LMD's job vacancies posted online job portals.

2. DiCoDe: Demanded Skills Diagnosis Project

Information is a valuable asset in the job search process for LMD and for LMS. For both types of actors the quality and kind of information regarding vacancies, salaries, skills, competencies, among others, are crucial for an efficient allocation of the jobs available in the labor market (Stigler, 1962). In a context of great heterogeneity of both jobs and workers (and where none has all the information), lowering the costs of finding work to achieve a "good match" can have effects on productivity (Mortensen, 2011).

On the other hand, achieving a good match between LMD and LMS can also result in wage segregation problems or access barriers for less qualified workers (David, 2001). Whereby, it is essential not only to facilitate an efficient assignment of positions but also to identify training lines in the most demanded skills so that more workers increase their chances of match.

In this context, DiCoDe arises as a system that tracks job vacancies that online job portals show for CDMX, downloading them in bulk and storing them systematically for subsequent analysis. In the Figure 1 we can see the amount of job offers published online in the year 2019-2020 in CDMX.

To do so, DiCoDe uses two type of bots, one to index all urls that contain a vacancy and the second one to visit and download its information. This is then stored, preserving its main text structure (html headings) such as name of the vacancy, location, date of publication, salary offered, time

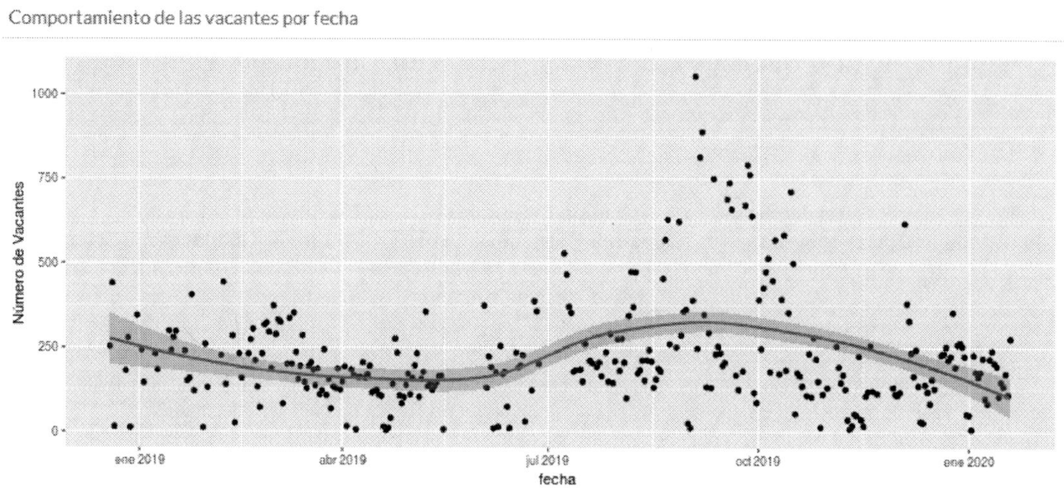

Figure 1: Number of vacancies published by year 2018-19 (screenshot from DiCoDe).

required, etc. Similar projects that take online job vacancies as a main source of information to analyze local labor markets have been developed in other countries of Latin America and the world (Altamirano et al., 2019; Amaral et al., 2018; Boselli et al., 2018). However, it is the first time that a project with these characteristics has been developed by the public sector in Mexico. It is important to emphasize that the DiCoDe System only uses data from vacancies offered online. Personal data of job applicants was not used for the system.

The main challenge is that each vacancy contains rich information, usually reported in an unstructured way (much of it in the "free text" section of each vacancy). Furthermore, employers use a variety of synonyms, ambiguous, redundant and imprecise language, which requires a detailed yet systematic NLP processing.

2.1. Collaboration academia and government

Faced with this challenge, STyFE contacted the Language Engineering Group (GIL) to find a solution based on the implementation of Language Technologies. The collaboration between academia and government allows the transfer of knowledge and technology for the benefit of citizens. The interdisciplinary work between the researchers and students of the GIL allowed the technological implementation to the challenge described.

We were asked to improve the performance of the DiCoDe system through the application of Language Technologies to: a) detect the macro-structure of job vacancies in CDMX and segment them by areas, b) improve the geographic location system by city hall, c) create dictionaries of the terms related to the competences, skills and abilities requested, d) obtain a classification of vacancies that allow structuring the database with categories reflecting CSA, e) improve the results and the processing time to perform text queries to the database.

3. Enhancing DiCoDe System

The enhancements imply the development of seven phases: 1) taxonomic information of job offers in CDMX, 2) design of a neural networks system to classify job offers, 3) implementation of an algorithm for improving the geographic location of the offers, 4) elaboration of a dictionary of vocabulary related to the topic, extracted form the data base, 5) building of a method based on regular expressions to automatically extract the features of the jobs, 6) implementation of dynamic filters for classification of offers, 7) identification of terms for free text searches.

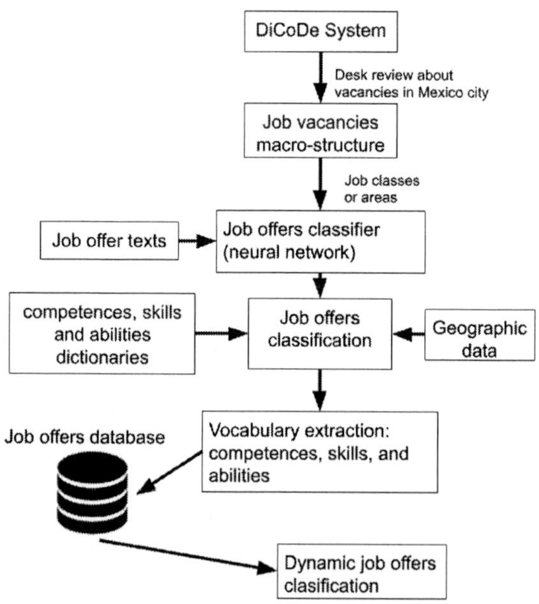

Figure 2: Structure of the system

3.1. Retrieving Taxonomic Information of job offers in CDMX

Determining the macro-structure of the set of job vacancies in CDMX is essential to know what types of occupations are offered to the inhabitants. A desk review suggests that some international occupational taxonomies (ISCO-08, 2012; SOC, 2018; ESCO, 2017) contain more occupations than actually apply in CDMX. Moreover, Mexico's official classification system SINCO (Hernández, 2018), developed by the national statistics office (INEGI) and that had been used by STyFE since DiCoDe's beginning, has the caveat that some occupational groups are not very frequent in the CDMX (e.g. coastal occupations, mining, etc), in addition, its classification system and vocabulary/jargon differs from the one used by LMD, or LMD does not post some type of occupations in job portals (e.g. fishermen).
The solution was to use the taxonomy of the Bumeran (Bumeran, 2020) job portal which groups 146 types of occupations into 23 main areas. The macro-structure of this site is built on the offers that employers publish with the geographical label "CDMX", therefore it represents the diversity of job vacancies found online.
This macro-structure of 23 categories grouping 146 types of occupations is an input for automatically classifying vacancies using a supervised learning algorithm. In the entry, the algorithm receives as input a set of job offers labeled with the categories of the Bumeran portal.

3.2. Neural Networks to classify job offers

We use a supervised learning approach with neural networks, using an LSTM architecture to build a job offers classifier based on the 23 classes mentioned above. These classes are: sales, human resources, technology, trades, administration, health, call center, legal, engineering, design, logistics, insurance, gastronomy, communication, secretary, finance, foreign trade, construction, marketing, production, education, management and mining.

3.2.1. Dataset

In order to train the classifier, we use a dataset with 979,956 examples, each one containing a job offer description text and its corresponding label. In Table 1, we show the details of the dataset:

Label	number of examples
Administration	124,349
Call center	152,820
Foreign trade	3,387
Communication	6,865
Construction	8,960
Design	9,897
Education	8,695
Financing	21,984
Gastronomy	20,995
Management	6,491
Engineering	14,521
Legal	10,004
Logistics	36,993
Marketing	31,519
Mining	635
Trades	56,931
Production	14,884
Human Resources	35,145
Health	21,501
Secretary	18,121
Insurance	0.9
Technology	87,105
Sales	277,197
Total	979,956

Table 1: Dataset details

3.2.2. Methodology

This section explains the processing that was carried out in the corpus to subsequently perform the classification task.

- Text normalization: Job offer texts were standardized to lowercase, and we put a dash if the text was empty.
- Stopwords removal.
- Punctuation symbols removal.
- Tokenization.

3.2.3. Neural network architecture

We use Keras library to build the model in a simple and fast way. Figure 3 shows a block diagram describing the neural network architecture:

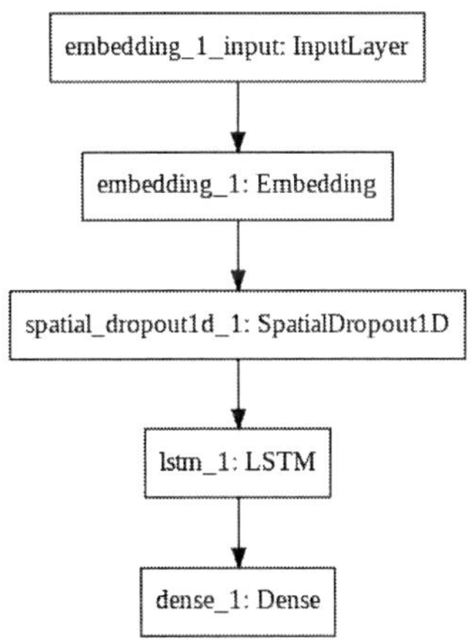

Figure 3: Neural network architecture

Embedding layer: It generates vector representations of words that capture semantic information from them.

Dropout layer: Set randomly a fraction of the input units to zero in each update during model training to avoid its overfitting.

LSTM layer: This layer allows the neural network to learn long-term dependencies.

Dense layer: This layer performs the activation function of the neural network, in this case, a softmax function.

Results are presented in Tables 2 and 3.

Label	Precision	Recall	F1	Support
Administration	0.95	0.94	0.94	24951
Call center	0.90	0.93	0.92	30578
Foreign trade	0.93	0.88	0.90	716
Communication	0.88	0.77	0.82	1396
Construction	0.94	0.92	0.93	1740
Design	0.96	0.93	0.94	2001
Education	0.92	0.93	0.92	1682
Financing	0.93	0.89	0.91	4396
Gastronomy	0.82	0.94	0.93	4313
Management	0.94	0.92	0.88	1321
Engineering	0.91	0.90	0.90	2073
Legal	0.89	0.95	0.92	2019
Logistics	0.92	0.95	0.94	7380
Marketing	0.93	0.92	0.93	6372
Mining	0.86	0.89	0.87	133
Trades	0.91	0.86	0.89	11331
Production	0.90	0.91	0.90	2943
Human Resources	0.95	0.94	0.94	6945
Health	0.95	0.93	0.94	4316
Secretary	0.89	0.89	0.89	3645
Insurance	0.91	0.90	0.90	2230
Technology	0.95	0.93	0.94	17537
Sales	0.94	0.94	0.94	55174

Table 2: Neural Network Results

Approach	Value
Cross Entropy	0.2399
Accuracy	0.9272
Precision	0.9437
Recall	0.9163
F1 measure	0.9298

Table 3: Neural Network Results (approaches)

3.2.4. Comparison experiments

Several experiments were carried out using different approaches in order to compare these results with the results from our proposed solution using F1-score as a metric evaluation. For all the experiments, we apply the same text preprocessing steps described in section 3.2.2.

3.2.5. Comparison results

In this section, we briefly describe the experiments and show the obtained results.

- FastText: This is a library created by Facebook, which is based on the Bag of Words model and it was improved using multilayer neural networks-based classifiers (Montañes Salas et al., 2017). Results obtained with FastText are shown in Table 4.

- Traditional machine learning algorithms: The performance of the job offers classifier was tested using the following algorithms: Support Vector Machine (SVM), Naive-bayes (NB), logistic regression (LR) and random forest (RF). Results obtained in these experiments are shown in Table 5.

Label	Precision	Recall	F1	Support
Administration	0.92	0.93	0.92	37318
Call center	0.88	0.92	0.90	45753
Foreign trade	0.94	0.79	0.86	1072
Comunication	0.89	0.67	0.76	2099
Construction	0.92	0.89	0.90	2643
Design	0.94	0.91	0.93	3040
Education	0.95	0.89	0.92	2592
Financing	0.92	0.86	0.89	6572
Gastronomy	0.92	0.92	0.92	6392
Management	0.82	0.80	0.81	1980
Engineering	0.91	0.86	0.88	4326
Legal	0.89	0.90	0.90	3039
Logistics	0.91	0.93	0.92	11044
Marketing	0.93	0.89	0.91	9553
Mining	1.00	0.56	0.72	190
Trades	0.88	0.84	0.86	17050
Production	0.89	0.86	0.88	4443
Human resources	0.94	0.92	0.93	10420
Health	0.94	0.91	0.92	6398
Secretary	0.91	0.85	0.88	5481
Insurance	0.92	0.85	0.89	3328
Technology	0.95	0.91	0.93	26206
Sales	0.91	0.94	0.92	83048

Table 4: FastText results

Classifier	Accuracy	Precision	Recall	F1-score
SVM	0.65	0.62	0.43	0.48
NB	0.49	0.32	0.15	0.16
LR	0.61	0.53	0.40	0.44
RF	0.58	0.66	0.29	0.36

Table 5: Traditional machine learning algorithm results

3.3. Improving the geographic location system

With the objective of geographically locating vacancies by city hall, we developed an algorithm to improve the geographic classification of job vacancies at the city hall level by tracking geographical elements that appear in the column of 'area' in the vacancy database. For this activity it was first necessary to conduct a study on CDMX's territorial demarcations. With this information a dictionary has been developed that has served as the basis for the algorithm design.

The denominations of each of the 16 different territorial demarcations of Mexico City have variants in everyday use. Among these variants can be cases of acronyms, abbreviations and apocopes.

To search for words that could be related to the city hall's offices, a dictionary composed of two elements was built:

1. A list of *colonias* (city halls' subdivisions) and neighborhoods with their zip codes.

2. A list composed of the different denominations of CDMX's city hall.

The algorithm uses the dictionary of *colonias*, neighborhoods and city halls. The dictionary searches the area within DiCoDe's database for each of the items in the dictionary and returns the city hall where it is when there are

coincidences. As a result the algorithm produces a file with the original fields plus that of the city hall's containing the algorithm's findings. Job offers that offer vacancies in different locations are treated as separate offers by location.
In Figure 4 we can see the result of the application of the algorithm, which allows us to know the number of vacancies published online in each city hall.

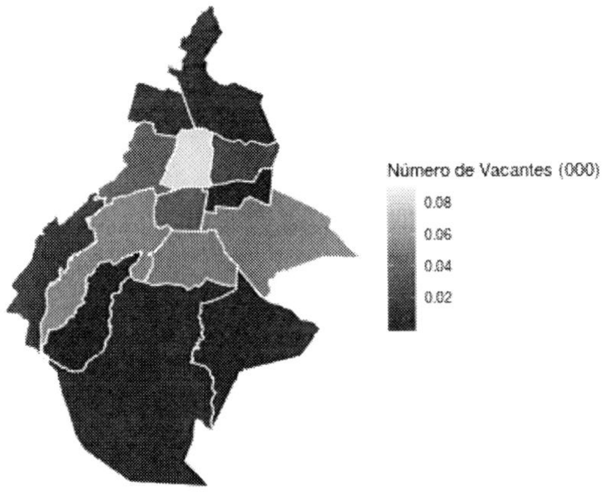

Figure 4: Vacancy number per City Hall (Map generated by DiCoDe System)

3.4. Extracting related vocabulary: competences, skills and abilities

The web portals that publish the job vacancies allow LMD actors to use a "free text" space for describing job duties, relevant skills, etc. In this field the specific requirements of the vacancy are detailed, without any restriction, so that each LMD actor writes the information differently, without following a preset template. Therefore, the names and distribution of the demanded CHD varies, resulting in the concepts being ambiguous and used interchangeably, so they are usually grouped into different items.
To enhance DiCoDe's robustness, Natural Language Processing (NLP) models are applied. To that purpose, the information found in each vacancy is classified into preestablished categories using a dictionary containing the competences, skills, and abilities, that was created ad-hoc to perform this task. It was constructed using the information found on the online job portals.
To this end, some basic concepts were defined in a first step: the dictionary, a semantic field and grammar. Then, the terms used by the OECD and the ILO on competence, dexterity, skill, requirement and capacity were revised, which allowed us to begin extracting dictionary entries. From here the categories were refined, which ended up being defined as follows:

Competence / skill: Knowledge of a specific activity or knowledge that encompasses both theory and practice and allows executing tasks. Ability to easily and accurately perform the tasks of an occupation that require physical movements.

Requirement: Competence, aptitude, knowledge or characteristic requested by an employer. It is generally a mandatory and a verifiable attribute and lacking it reduces the probability of getting the job.

Capacity: Cognitive process related to information management, accessible when carrying out a work task.

Experience: Practice acquired from the exercise of an activity during a certain period of time.

Function: Activity that a person performs within a job.

In this way, the final categories, their definitions and the analysis of semantic features allowed the concrete and real determination of what Mexican employers consider when referring to each of the categories.

3.5. Sorting job offers to structure the database

At this stage we perform a class and category detection algorithm through the search for patterns in the free text of job vacancies. For this activity we mainly use regular expressions. In NLP tasks the use of regular expressions for the patterns' detection in text is very frequent for subsequent analysis and treatment. The extraction of information is the process of locating portions of a text given that they contain information relevant to the needs of a user and provide such information in a manner appropriate to their process.
To enhance DiCoDe's efficiency and accelerate its classification process we have decided to use regular expressions in Perl 6.0, which contains a standardized and standard set of regular expressions, quite powerful and easy to understand. We decided to implement our solution in Perl's modules, because it's open source, free and portable.

ID Job offer identifier (unique sequential integer)

GENDER Requested gender: male | female | indistinct, if it exists

SALARY Salary offered (if any)

AGE Required age (if any)

HOURS Working hours: in hours, full-time | part-time, days of the week

SCHEDULE Field that sometimes contains additional salary information, schedule

DEDICATION Field that sometimes informs about full time, part time, etc.

TEXT Field that contains the information of the company and the offer, if it exists.

For the extraction of the fields corresponding to competence / ability, capacity, experience, requirements and functions a python program was used in which the following process applies:

- Preprocessing of the text: the free text corresponding to job offers is put into lowercase, accents are removed with the aim of avoiding repetitions of words and possible writing errors and vacancies are rearranged in a line.

- Search of fields of interest: from a collection of regular expressions, the areas mentioned above are searched in the previously processed text, these are: competence / ability, capacity, experience, requirements and functions.

- Writing output file: once the fields of interest are extracted from the free text of the offers, they are stored in a csv file with the following columns: text, competence / skill, ability, experience, requirements and functions.

3.6. Dynamic vacancy classification

We perform a filtering algorithm that allows a dynamic classification of job vacancies, creating a structured database for DiCoDe. The algorithm allows identifying those fields mentioned above.
To carry out the above, the following is done:

1. Take the first of the variables and display a list with the different elements it contains numbered by their respective indexes.

2. Ask the user to indicate the number of items he wants to take, from the list displayed, to add to the filter.

3. Based on the number of items selected by the user, you are asked to add the index number of the first item, of the subsequent ones.

4. The console takes the following variable and will display a list with the different elements it contains numbered by their respective indexes.

5. The process is repeated until the filters are created for all the variables

6. Finally, indicate the number of vacancies selected with the filters and the base where they were stored.

3.7. Identification of terms for free text searches

We build an algorithm for identification of terms for free text searches on job offers present in the DiCoDe database. The developed algorithm allows to obtain all those requirements belonging to an area of the macro-taxonomy used for the classification of job offers; This means that it is possible to look for the competences, desired experience, requirements, functions to perform, requested sex, age range and salary belonging to a certain area.
The algorithm receives as input two things: the area on which the search will be conducted and a database where an initial filtering will be carried out to obtain only the job offers that correspond to the area of interest.
Then the values for the columns of sex, salary, age, schedule, competence / ability, ability, experience, requirements and functions of each job offer belonging to the area of interest are obtained, and adds them to a list where there are no repeated elements .
Finally, a file in a standard .xlsx format is returned that contains the values of sex, salary, age, schedule, competence / ability, ability, experience, requirements and functions of each offer in the selected area.

4. Conclusion and perspectives

By tracking and analyzing vacancies posted on job portals, DiCoDe promises to contribute to evidence-based policy making, specially those aspects regarding training and skills development. To that end, the collaboration between STyFE and GIL has led to fruitful preliminary results. The classification task approached with a neural network has retrieved very satisfactory results with 1,000.000 records and 23 classes, taken from one of the portals.
Preliminary results also suggest that this methodology can be easily adaptable to classify vacancies to both other macro-strcutures and to other geographical areas beyond CDMX. These results have contribute to reduce computing time that, given an accumulated stock of about 5.6 million vacancies, has proven crucial. Moreover, the developed methodology and algorithms not only contribute to overcome the challenges faced by DiCoDe but also to extend some of the know-how to other activities undertaken by STyFE.
An appropriate evaluation should be performed to test both efficiency and correctness of classifications into macro-structures and CSA categories, while also robustness and sensitivity analysis to varying inputs is also pending.
With the implementation of language technologies on the job vacancies data, DiCoDe is expected to reduce information asymmetries in different analytical categories (occupation types, CSA, etc) thereby making information more accessible to job seekers, employers and other actors, including STyFE itself. In this sense, it is expected to foster a more efficient job search and match, while also allowing an enhanced identification of training needs to allow, for more equitable job placement opportunities, inter alia.
It could be interesting in the future to implement hybrid strategies in order to make a best match between the job vacancies and candidates (Kessler et al., 2012).
Finally, we also contemplate in the future the use of Automatic Text Summarization techniques, which could generate relevant syntheses (groups) of groups of job vacancies (Torres-Moreno, 2014).

5. Acknowledgements

The project was supported by an agreeement (IISGCONV-084-2019) UNAM-STyFE (Mexico). J.-M. Torres-Moreno was partially financed by the *Laboratoire Informatique d'Avignon* (LIA), Université d'Avignon (France).

6. Bibliographical References

Altamirano, A., Azuara, O., González, S., Ospino, C., Sánchez, D., and Torres, J. (2019). Tendencias de las ocupaciones en américa latina y el caribe 2000-2015. Technical Report IDB-TN-1821, Banco Interamericano de Desarrollo.

Amaral, N., Eng, N., Ospino, C., Pagés, C., Rucci, G., and Williams, N. (2018). How far can your skills take you. Technical Report IDB-TN-01501, Banco Interamericano de Desarrollo.

Boselli, R., Cesarini, M., Marrara, S., Mercorio, F., Mezzanzanica, M., Pasi, G., and Viviani, M. (2018). Wolmis: a labor market intelligence system for classifying web job vacancies. *Journal of Intelligent Information Systems*, 51(3):477–502.

Bumeran. (2020). Bumeran: empleos destacados en méxico. https://www.bumeran.com.mx/. Accessed: 2020-02-16.

David, H. (2001). Wiring the labor market. *Journal of Economic Perspectives*, 15(1):25–40.

ESCO. (2017). European skills/competences, qualifications and occupations. Technical report, European Union. https://ec.europa.eu/esco/portal.

Hart, O. D. (1983). Optimal labour contracts under asymmetric information: An introduction. *The Review of Economic Studies*, 50(1):3–35.

Hernández, C. (2018). Ocupaciones laborales: clasificaciones, taxonomías y ontologías para los mercados laborales del siglo xxi. Technical report, Observatorio laboral: http://www.observatoriolaboral.gob.mx/.

INEGI. (2020). Encuesta nacional de ocupación y empleo (enoe), población de 15 años y más de edad. https://www.inegi.org.mx/programas/enoe/15ymas/default.html#Tabulados. Accessed: 2020-02-16.

ISCO-08. (2012). International standard classification of occupations. isco-08. Technical report, International Labor Office.

Kessler, R., Béchet, N., Roche, M., Torres-Moreno, J.-M., and El-Bèze, M. (2012). A hybrid approach to managing job offers and candidates. *Information Processing & Management*, 6(48):1124–1135.

Montañes Salas, R. M., del Hoyo Alonso, R., Vea-Murguía Merck, J., Aznar Gimeno, R., and Lacueva-Pérez, J. (2017). FastText as an alternative to using Deep Learning in small corpus.

Mortensen, D. T. (2011). Markets with search friction and the dmp model. *American Economic Review*, 101(4):1073–91.

OIT. (2020). Centro interamericano para el desarrollo del conocimiento en la formación profesional. https://www.oitcinterfor.org/taxonomy/term/3366. Accessed: 2020-02-16.

SOC. (2018). Standard occupational classification. Technical report, US Bureau of Labor Statistics.

Stigler, G. J. (1962). Information in the labor market. *Journal of political economy*, 70(5, Part 2):94–105.

STyFE. (2019). Análisis de las intersecciones entre la oferta y la demanda laboral en la Ciudad de México. Technical report, Secretaría del Trabajo y Fomento al Empleo. https://www.trabajo.cdmx.gob.mx.

Torres-Moreno, J.-M. (2014). *Automatic Text Summarization*. Wiley, London.

Proceedings of the First workshop on Language Technologies for Government and Public Admnistration (LT4Gov), pages 22–27
Language Resources and Evaluation Conference (LREC 2020), Marseille, 11–16 May 2020
© European Language Resources Association (ELRA), licensed under CC-BY-NC

Research & Innovation Activities' Impact Assessment: The Data4Impact System

Ioanna Grypari, Dimitris Pappas, Natalia Manola, Haris Papageorgiou
Athena Research & Innovation Center
Artemidos 6 & Epidavrou 15125, Marousi, Greece
{igrypari, dpappas, nmanola, haris} @ athenarc.gr

Abstract

We present the Data4Impact (D4I) platform, a novel end-to-end system for evidence-based, timely and accurate monitoring and evaluation of research and innovation (R&I) activities. Using the latest technological advances in Human Language Technology (HLT) and our data-driven methodology, we build a novel set of indicators in order to track funded projects and their impact on science, the economy and the society as a whole, during and after the project life-cycle. We develop our methodology by targeting Health-related EC projects from 2007 to 2019 to produce solutions that meet the needs of stakeholders (mainly policy-makers and research funders). Various D4I text analytics workflows process datasets and their metadata, extract valuable insights and estimate intermediate results and metrics, culminating in a set of robust indicators that the users can interact with through our dashboard, the D4I Monitor (available at monitor.data4impact.eu). Therefore, our approach, which can be generalized to different contexts, is multidimensional (technology, tools, indicators, dashboard) and the resulting system can provide an innovative solution for public administrators in their policy-making needs related to RDI funding allocation.

Keywords: HLT, NLP, RDI, impact evaluation, policy-making, public administration

1. Monitoring, Evaluation & Policy-making in R&I Activities

As the number of programmes available for financing Research & Innovation (R&I) activities has been growing, so has the need to update the monitoring and evaluation of such activities. Traditional assessment systems are costly, rely disproportionately on the self-declared performance from project participants, and limit the relevant evaluation period to the project's lifetime.

Moreover, the accurate assessment of awarded R&I projects is essential for future policy-making. Answers to questions such as:

"What lessons can be learned from past projects? Which research areas are emerging? How much have I, as a funder, invested in those areas compared to other funders, and how "crowded" are they? What "type" of projects create innovations that reach the market quickly? Which companies are still innovating in the same field that they received funding for? Which organisations play a key role in the diffusion of technology? What are the most important research communities and how are they spread out across countries and sectors? What are the characteristics of projects whose outputs reach the average person faster? What issues do people care about?"

among others, are key in understanding the potential impact of R&I activities, allow for evidence-based policy-making and, in principle, for an "optimal" allocation of funding resources.

In fact, there is a wide range of research on the different possible R&I impact avenues and their estimation techniques, the most established of which comes from scientometrics. Nevertheless, technological advancements in the areas of HLT have brought forth the capabilities to update these traditionally-used tools and significantly augment our approach with more varied sources of data and frontier technologies.

There is, thus, an opportunity to build monitoring systems that are, to a large extent, automated and offer accurate, timely, granular and multidimensional estimates of the performance of R&I activities and their effects on the society at large. This is the mission of the Data4Impact (hereafter D4I) platform, which we present in this showcase.

There is limited literature on evidence-based end-to-end systems. STAR metrics (Largent and Lane, 2012)is a US infrastructure that tracks a wide range of administrative and other data to analyze input, output and outcomes of federal R&D investments. Corpus Viewer (Pérez-Fernández et al., 2019), a Spanish initiative, uses HLT technologies on text and metadata (mainly from patents, scientific publications and grant proposals) to build indicators for policy evaluation, and additionally offers tools for policy implementation and identification of cases of double funding and fraud in proposals.

Although *complementary* to the D4I approach, there are several differences among the three systems; the most prominent being the sources and coverage of indicators. In fact, to the best of our knowledge, our platform is the only one that offers a holistic approach and at this level of breadth, supporting indicators from input to the different possible dimensions of impact.

Using HLT and other methodologies, we extract pertinent information from project reports, publications, patents, company websites, policy documents (clinical guidelines), products (drugs) and traditional and social media and link them across different entities (projects, topics, countries, funders, and so on). This results in a rich database of analytics and indicators that can be "sliced" across different dimensions according to the needs of the policy-makers and other stakeholders.

Moreover, our platform accommodates the D4I Monitor,[1] a BI tool that allows us to map a complex set of methodologies and analytics onto a user friendly dashboard with interactive visualizations of indicators and customization capabilities.

In Section 2, we briefly describe the datasets, methodology and resulting indicators of the workflows of the D4I end-to-end platform, and proceed, in Section 3, to present the dashboard. In Section 4, we conclude.

2. D4I Processing Workflows & Indicators

Data4Impact is a Horizon 2020 project[2] aimed at addressing the mission described in the Introduction. Namely, we built end-to-end workflows that use the latest technologies in Machine/Deep Learning to create a novel and rich set of indicators that are granular, timely and track a funded project's performance and its impact, well after the end of its life-cycle.

We broke down the monitoring needs of a project into five stages: input (at the initial setup of the project), throughput/output (during/at the end of the project) and academic, economic and societal impact (mostly after the end of the project capturing its mid- and long-term impact). We developed our methodology by focusing on EC projects in health and health-related fields in FP7 and H2020 programmes. Importantly, experts in the particular sector guided us to the right data sources for identifying the input-to-impact story. Our approach is generalizable to other policy areas, conditioned upon the human-in-the-loop process to guarantee good coverage of impact scenarios.

2.1. Projects

In order to track the input-to-impact process across projects, we start by examining the textual content of project-related documents (associated call, proposal, reports, deliverables, publications and patents created in the context of the project, and so on). We use a wealth of NLP methods in the steps of our workflows.

First, we segment the content of project reports and publication abstracts (i.e. using its *rhetorical structure*) and isolate the sections and publication zones that relate to the contributions, results and impact of each project and research team. Next, we conduct entity recognition and keyterm extraction using SGRank (Danesh et al., 2015) to help define the work conducted and subject matter of each document, and to build graphs that depict the correlations between entities. This allows us to explore spatial/temporal trends and patterns across projects. Further, we apply our innovation extraction framework that annotates innovation statements into a pre-defined set of domain-independent (e.g., publication, patent, employment), domain-related (e.g., device, diagnostic tool) and domain-dependent (e.g., drug, treatment, clinical trial) insights.

Moreover, it is important to note that disease mentions along with MeSH terms and other established disease classification schemes, like the ICD, are leveraged to automatically classify projects according to research areas. Additionally, and with the objective to provide multidimensional KPI analytics, metadata are taken into account. Specifically, financial data about the cost of each project along with the budget distribution per participant are considered. Moreover, data relevant to each organisation participating in the project, such as the country it is based and its type, i.e., whether it is a research organisation, a university or a company, is gathered and leveraged to construct collaboration networks that help quantify the collaboration and diffusion of technology (using different centrality measures) between the beneficiaries. Merging this work with the extracted data analytics and classification enable us to create a wealth of indicators that can be compared across different types of entities such as funders, time, participating organisations, etc.

To track the evolution of innovations and measure the impact of projects past their life-cycle, we target different data sources. First, we measure the technological value of patents produced in projects by counting their forward and backward citations,[3] and the technological value of publications by examining how many patents cite them.

Second, to build economic impact indicators we crawl the websites of the private-for-profit beneficiaries in the projects. We apply our NLP workflows and pipelines as described above, adapted to the task, isolate their current innovation activities and outputs, and quantitatively relate them to those produced in the context of their EC projects. In particular, we propose a novel method to proxy the commercialization of projects' innovations by the companies, the *uptake score*, by creating a graph semantically linking the keyterms from the three types of documents (project reports, publications, company websites).

Third, to examine the societal impact of projects, we collect policy documents (clinical guidelines), clinical trials and data related to drugs linked to projects. We analyse the contextual fragments related to cited references and other extracted data to construct indicators that measure the reach of the project innovations to the society via generating health-related impact.

[1] Under development and available at monitor.data4impact.eu.

[2] cordis.europa.eu/project/id/770531

[3] I.e., the number of patents a particular patents cites, vs. the number of patents that cite the particular patent

2.2. Topics

Understanding the need of policy-makers to assess the input-to-impact process also from a "bird's eye" view, we worked on the training and development of topic models. The Multi-View Topic Modelling framework consists of several components targeting information extraction, semantic annotation and, most importantly, automated multi-dimensional analysis based on an innovative multi-view probabilistic topic modelling engine (Metaxas and Ioannidis, 2017). We took a large sample of health-related research and used this bottom up approach to divide the field into topics that were manually validated and labeled by a field expert, and placed into generic, major categories. The output of the topic modelling algorithm also provides us with project-topic associations. This allows us to connect all the project-level data, and the previously-described indicators, with their topic distribution. It is also the key in the construction of "non-traditional" academic impact indicators that measure the timeliness, investment potential and exclusivity of research funding, amongst other variables, by comparing the strength of a topic (research volume) across different funders and the entire (academic) health domain. Further, the richness of the topic modelling output, together with the metadata available, allow us to create topic-based similarity indicators that enable us to compare different entities (e.g., countries) according to the topic distribution of their research output.

Lastly, to expand our analysis of societal-level indicators, we pick a subset of "essential" topics (determined using project extracted innovations and the insight of a field expert), and performed relevant searches on traditional and social media.

In particular, we gauge the societal relevance of these topics, by creating indicators based on their media buzz as well as on different characteristics of twitter conversations related to them. The latter is also augmented with visualizations that depict the evolution of twitter discussions. (Lorentzen et al., 2019).

2.3. The Input-to-Impact Story

This rich set of metrics and indicators is thus supported by establishing links among different types of entities at a granular level. First, by aggregating hierarchically upwards we can examine R&I activities and their impact at the Project, Call, Programme and Funder (e.g., the EC) level.[4] Second, using the project metadata we can refine the results further and filter them for particular organizations (beneficiaries), countries and over time.

Moreover, we are also able to track R&I activities from input to impact at the very fine level of the topic (or aggregated to a major category or the entire health field). This offers a different view of monitoring that is well-suited for comparisons across different entities as it abstracts from the programmatic structure of funding schemes, and can also offer a rich and novel set of indicators that rely on topics and their characteristics. Further, through the project-topic associations, topic-based indicators can be also refined and examined for particular organizations (other funders or project participants), countries and over time.

Therefore, one of the strengths of the D4I indicators, and the underlying workflows, lies on the fact that the input-to-impact story of R&I activities can be unfolded in two ways: via projects or via topics (and the entities hierarchically above each).

Lastly, these novel indicators, in combination with traditionally used ones, can provide policy-makers with the quantitative information needed to conduct an in-depth and well-rounded assessment of various investment/funding opportunities by examining the correlations of metrics and project characteristics across different project stages. In other words, these indicators can be used in a statistical analysis not only to answer such questions as the ones presented in Section 1, but also to formally show the interplay among them.[5]

3. D4I Monitor

Given the complexity of the processing workflows and the various data sources, and in order to maximize the reach of the newly developed indicators, it is essential to create a flexible and user-friendly dashboard in order to communicate the results to policy-makers. This is the starting point of the D4I Monitor.

Figure 1: D4I Monitor - Landing Page

The D4I Monitor is an end-to-end Business Intelligence data and visualization tool that can be integrated to third-party platforms. It consolidates the outputs of the different modules of the D4I platform and allows policy operators to interact with and download visualizations and indicators for each of the five stages of input-to-impact described above.

[4]This is the particular hierarchy followed by the EC projects; in general, our approach is adjustable to other funding structures.

[5]As a simple example, one can examine if funding research on emerging topics could also mean contributing in the creation of innovations that not only reach the market quickly but also are successful, in the sense of people knowing and using them.

We organise the data on the dashboard to fit the needs of our stakeholders. In particular, a user can view a report, i.e., a series of visualizations displayed over five input-to-impact tabs, by first selecting either a topic (or major category, or field), or an item from their portfolio (Search Bar in Figure 2). The latter is populated with projects, calls, programmes and organisations that the user selects, conditioned on data access rights (Figure 3).[6]

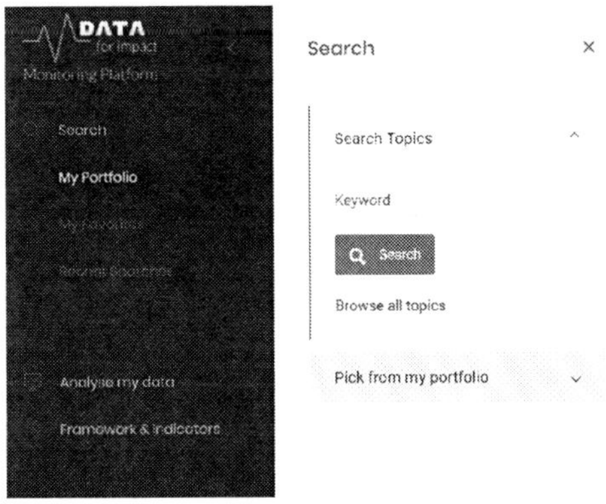

Figure 2: D4I Monitor - Side Bar & Search Bar

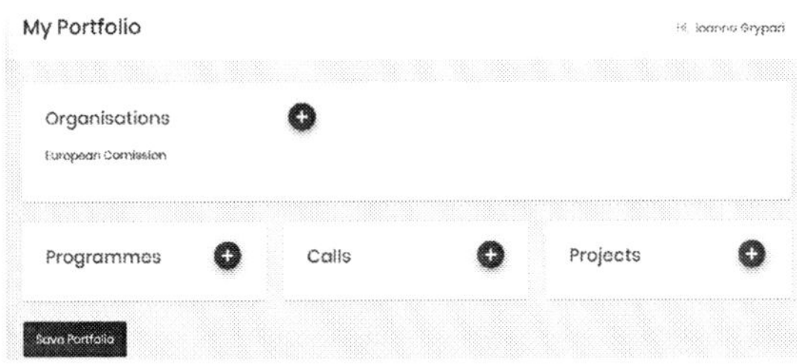

Figure 3: D4I Monitor - Portfolio

In order to use all pertinent data we have available, at the topic search, we match the word typed by a user not only to the name of a topic, but also to the associated keywords/phrases from the topic models and rank topics by quality of match using the corresponding keyword weights. As an example, Figure 4 displays the results that come up after searching for the keyword "malaria."

Once a particular entity is selected and the report is displayed, the user can take advantage of our multidimensional analysis by filtering the entire report further by the country, participating organisation or time range of interest (Figure 5).

In the report itself, each interactive visualization presents the values of one or more indicators. A user can filter

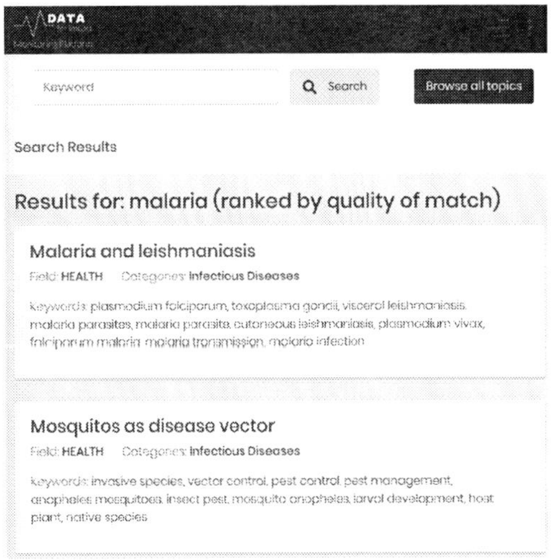

Figure 4: D4I Monitor - "malaria" Search Results

Figure 5: D4I Monitor - Filtering (Not Active)

for particular entities and hover to view values of interest. There is the option to download the entire report in PDF and each visualization separately in PNG (the filtered/zoomed-in image), and the data behind it in CSV or JSON file formats (Figure 6).

Further features are being built so that the dashboard can meet the requirements of a go-to monitoring tool for R&I activities. In particular, users will be able to save and monitor different entities, receive updates, and request to have their own data analyzed and the results uploaded on the platform (Side Bar in Figure 2). In addition, the D4I Monitor is flexibly built so that it can accommodate more fields and indicators.

There are currently pilot studies underway, most recently with policy-makers working on rare diseases, to continue

[6]Given a different funding structure (e.g., personal grants), the portfolio would be adjusted to list the corresponding funding levels.

the improvement of the dashboard, the indicators and the underlying technologies.

4. Conclusion

In summary, the D4I platform brings together the information from a variety of sources and applies state-of-the-art methods to derive meaningful, timely and reproducible indicators linked across different entities. The developed end-to-end system allows stakeholders to monitor and evaluate their funding schemes and conduct data-driven policy-making. Our end-product, the D4I Monitor, is a user-friendly and agile platform that warrants ease of access of the results to policy-makers and guarantees the continued improvement of their policies.

5. Acknowledgements

Data4Impact has received funding from the European Union's Horizon 2020 research and innovation programme under grant agreement No 770531. The authors would like to thank all the consortium partners of Data4Impact for a fruitful and rewarding collaboration, namely PPMI, Fraunhofer ISI, CNR, University of Borås and Qualia SA.

6. Bibliographical References

Danesh, S., Sumner, T., and Martin, J. H. (2015). SGRank: Combining Statistical and Graphical Methods to Improve the State of the Art in Unsupervised Keyphrase Extraction. In *Proceedings of the Fourth Joint Conference on Lexical and Computational Semantics, SEM 2015*, pages 117–126.

Eklund, J., Gunnarsson Lorenzen, D., and Nelhans, G. (2019). Mesh Classification of Clinical Guidelines Using Conceptual Embeddings of References. In *17th International International Conference on Scientometrics and Informetrics, ISSI 2019*, volume 2, pages 859 — 864.

Feidenheimer, A. and Stanciauskas, V. (2019). Developing KPI's for Impact for Institutions and (Inter)national Policies. In *Impact of Science 2019*. Presentation.

Fergadis, A., Baziotis, C., Pappas, D., Papageorgiou, H., and Potamianos, A. (2018). Hierarchical Bi-directional Attention-based RNNs for Supporting Document Classification on Protein–protein Interactions Affected by Genetic Mutations. *Database*, 2018.

Grypari, I., Nelhans, G., and Stanciauskas, V. (2019). Application of Big Data in Scientometrics. In *17th International Conference on Scientometrics and Informetrics, ISSI 2019*. Workshop.

Gurell, J. and Nelhans, G. (2018). A National CRIS in Sweden – a Developer's and a Researcher's Perspective. In *CRIS2018: 14th International Conference on Current Research Information Systems*. Keynote Address.

Largent, M. A. and Lane, J. I. (2012). STAR METRICS and the Science of Science Policy. *Review of Policy Research*, 29(3):431–438.

Lorentzen, D., Eklund, J., Nelhans, G., and Ekström, B. (2019). On the Potential for Detecting Scientific Issues and Controversies on Twitter: A Method for Investigation Conversations Mentioning Research. In *17th International Conference on Scientometrics and Informetrics, ISSI 2019*, pages 2189 – 2198.

Metaxas, O. and Ioannidis, Y. (2017). Multi-View Topic Modelling on Text-Augmented Heterogeneous Information Networks. Under submission.

Nelhans, G., Vlachos, E., and Vigne, M. (2019). Towards a Responsible Institute Impact Assessment. In *Liber Conference 2019*. Presentation.

Pérez-Fernández, D., Arenas-García, J., Samy, D., Padilla-Soler, A., and Gómez-Verdejo, V. (2019). Corpus Viewer: NLP and ML-based Platform for Public Policy Making and Implementation. *Procesamiento del Lenguaje Natural*, 63:193 – 196.

Pukelis, L. and Stanciaukas, V. (2018). Big Data Approaches to Estimating the Impact of EU Research Funding on Innovation Development. In *STI 2018 Conference Proceedings*, pages 429 – 435.

Pukelis, L. and Stanciauskas, V. (2019). Opportunities and Limitations of Using Artificial Neural Networks in Social Science Research. *Politologija*, 94(2):356 – 380.

Pukelis, L. (2019). Using Internet Data to Compliment Traditional Innovation Indicators. In *International Conference on Public Policy (ICPP4)*. Presentation.

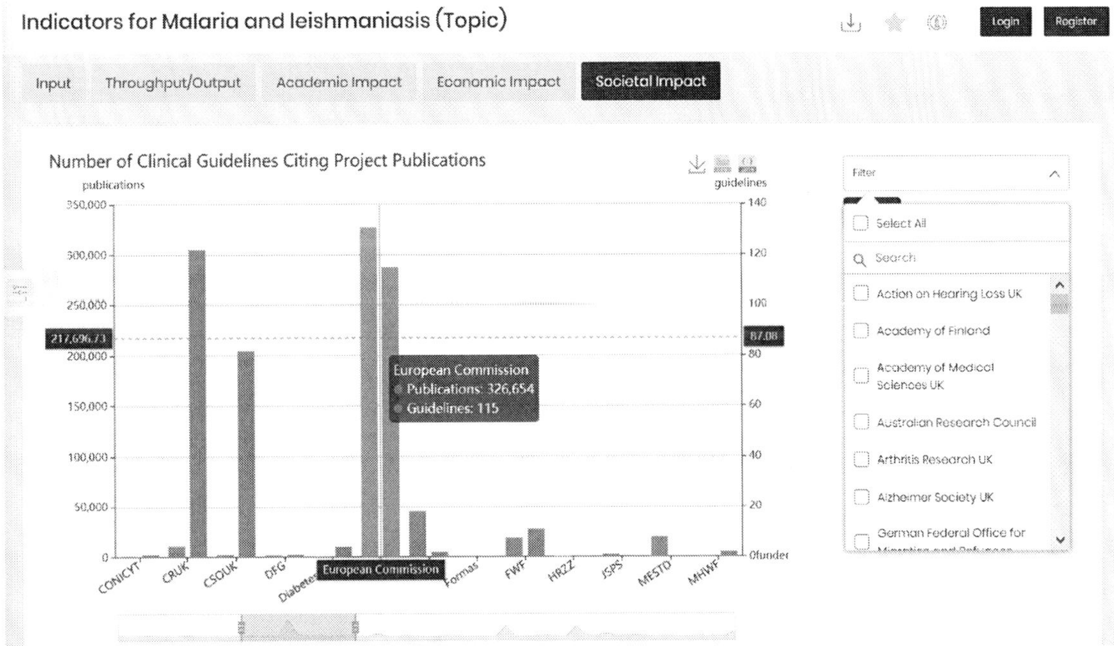

Figure 6: D4I Monitor - Sample from a Report

Proceedings of the First workshop on Language Technologies for Government and Public Admnistration (LT4Gov), pages 28–31
Language Resources and Evaluation Conference (LREC 2020), Marseille, 11–16 May 2020
© European Language Resources Association (ELRA), licensed under CC-BY-NC

The Austrian Language Resource Portal for the Use and Provision of Language Resources in a Language Variety by Public Administration – a Showcase for Collaboration between Public Administration and a University

Barbara Heinisch, Vesna Lušicky
Centre for Translation Studies, University of Vienna, Austria
Gymnasiumstraße 50, 1190 Vienna
{barbara.heinisch, vesna.lusicky}@univie.ac.at

Abstract

The Austrian Language Resource Portal (*Sprachressourcenportal Österreichs*) is Austria's central platform for language resources in the area of public administration. It focuses on language resources in the Austrian variety of the German language. As a product of the cooperation between a public administration body and a university, the Portal contains various language resources (terminological resources in the public administration domain, a language guide, named entities based on open public data, translation memories, etc.). German is a pluricentric language that considerably varies in the domain of public administration due to different public administration systems. Therefore, the Austrian Language Resource Portal stresses the importance of language resources specific to a language variety, thus paving the way for the re-use of variety-specific language data for human language technology, such as machine translation training, for the Austrian standard variety.

Keywords: Language varieties, language resource collection, public administration

1. Introduction

The Austrian Language Resource Portal (*Sprachressourcenportal Österreichs*, sprachressourcen.at) is Austria's central platform for language resources in the area of public administration. It focuses on language resources in the Austrian variety of the German language and provides language aids to enable communication about Austrian public administration on a national and European level in English. The Austrian Language Resource Portal aims at offering a sustainable and extendable platform for the provision of both human-readable and machine-readable language resources for multilingual communication on public administration, and language technologies tailored to the Austrian variety of the German language, such as machine translation engines. The main target groups consist of public administration staff, translators, interpreters and the public. The Portal is the tangible result of a long-term cooperation between the Austrian Armed Forces Language Institute as part of the Austrian public administration and the Centre for Translation Studies of the University of Vienna. The language resources that are made available via the Portal are the product of a cooperation between governmental translators and terminologists and scholars from the field of translation and terminology studies.

Before elaborating on the contents of the Austrian Language Resource Portal, it is important to illustrate the significance of an individual language resource portal for the Austrian variety of the German language.

2. The Austrian Variety of the German Language

German is considered to be a pluricentric language, "i.e. a language with several interacting centers, each providing a national variety with at least some of its own (codified) norms" (Clyne, 1995: 20). In the localization industry, there is a similar notion of a locale, i.e. a group of characteristics, information or rules related to linguistic, cultural, domain-specific and geographic conventions in a target group (DIN ISO 18587:2018). These conventions differ between the locales.

2.1 German as a Pluricentric Language

German as a pluricentric language has three standard varieties (Schmidlin, 2011), with Austrian German being one of the three codified standard forms (German, Austrian, Swiss) and, therefore, a diatopic variety.

German is the (co-)official language in seven countries or parts of European countries (Austria, Belgium, Germany, Italy, Liechtenstein, Luxembourg, and Switzerland). The Austrian variety of the German language differs in several respects from other varieties of German (Wiesinger, 1988), whereas lexical differences are the most pronounced and obvious ones. In several cases, words have the same meaning in Germany and Austria, but in Austria these words have an additional meaning as well. If lexical items are unique to Austria, they are called Austriacisms. Other differences between the German and Austrian standard varieties, in addition to the lexical ones, include pronunciation, the grammatical gender of nouns (e.g. 'the yoghurt', which has a masculine gender in the German variety "*der Joghurt*" and a neuter gender in the Austrian (and Swiss) variety "*das Joghurt*") or the use of tenses or prepositions (Wiesinger, 1996).

Before Austria joined the European Union, language and language identity were at the center of a public debate. This resulted in an additional document to Austria's accession treaty (Protocol no.10) that lists 23 Austrian expressions for food (e.g. *Topfen, Marille*) that must be used in the EU legislation. Although the goal of this list seems to be mainly to address the concerns of the population before joining the EU (de Cillia & Wodak, 2002), it is still significant as it is the only EU contract document granting a special status to a language variety in the EU.

2.2 Language-variety-specific Terminology

Terminology may also be different between language varieties. This may cause misunderstandings due to diverging concepts of a term. Examples for the German language are, among others, food terminology (Schmidlin 2011) and legal and administrative terminology (Wissik

2013; Lohaus 2000). The diversity in administrative and legal terminology arises from different legal systems (de Groot, 1999). Therefore, the (terminological) difference between the Austrian and German language variety of German is more than a word list, i.e. the list of Austriacisms, which was demanded by Austria during its accession to the European Union (Schreiber, 2002; Markhardt 2002; EU 1995). Major misunderstandings may, of course, originate from terminology, but these two standard varieties also differ with regard to syntax, grammar, morphology, etc. (Wiesinger, 1996).
In the domain of public administration, misunderstandings between speakers of different German varieties may arise since the related terms refer to different administration systems. These include terms such as *Magistrat, Bezirk, Landeshauptmann* or *Landeshauptfrau, Bezirksinspektor* (Heinisch, 2020). The terms *Landeshauptmann* or *Landeshauptfrau* are used in Austria (and some parts of Italy), but are not used in Germany or Switzerland to refer to the head of a *Bundesland* (provincial government). Another example is the German translation of the term *district*. If it is translated as *Kreis*, it rather refers to the German administrative subdivision. Misunderstandings may arise if (Austrian) readers are not aware of the meaning of *Kreis* since they may be rather used to *Bezirk*.

3. The Portal

The Austrian Language Resource Portal understands itself as a user-oriented catalog for the Austrian variety of the German language in the public administration domain. It does not replace existing language resource repositories but presents language resources (LRs) and language technologies (LTs) specific to the Austrian variety of the German language. Here, the usability for the target group of public administration staff, translators, interpreters and terminologists and the aim of increasing the visibility of the Austrian language variety are key. Moreover, it presents the results of various LR and LT projects related to the Austrian German variety on one portal.
The primary users are specialized translators and staff working with the Austrian public administration who communicate in German, and (occasionally) also in English. In addition, the Portal caters to LT developers and natural language processing (NLP) researchers in need for terminological datasets in this domain.
The Austrian Language Resource Portal contains the following language resources and technologies in the area of Austrian public administration and related information:

3.1 Public Administration Terminology

Terminology is an important language resource. Therefore, a crucial component of the Austrian Language Resource Portal is a bilingual terminological database containing terminology used in public administration in Austria.
The terminological resource entitled *Fachglossar Österreichische Verwaltung. Deutsch – Englisch* (glossary of public administration) covers terminology in this domain in German and English. It contains terminology from the areas of Austrian public law, legislation and executive authorities. It is aimed at providing a terminological resource targeted at language professionals, such as translators and interpreters. Since it is tailored to the peculiarities of the Austrian public administration system, the bilingual terminological resource is aimed at offering internationally comprehensible and transparent English terms since there is hardly equivalence of concepts.
The terminology is standardized by an informal working group of translators and terminologists employed with the Austrian federal ministries (*Arbeitsgruppe Gouvernementaler Übersetzungs- und Terminologiedienste*, ARG GUT). These governmental translators and terminologists joined forces to exchange experiences and create language resources under the aegis of the Austrian Armed Forces Language Institute, such as the glossary of public administration, which is available in different human-readable and machine-readable formats, such as .pdf, .csv or .tbx. The work on the terminological resource also revealed inter-ministerial terminological differences such as those related to internal divisions and subdivisions. Therefore, a prescriptive approach was adopted. This bilingual glossary contains 696 entries covering administrative bodies and institutions in Austria, as well as administrative procedures and processes.

3.1.1 Collection of Variety-specific Language Resources for Machine Translation Training

A collection of language resources in the public administration domain for the Austrian variety of German on the Portal stems from the EU Council Presidency Translator project. The EU Council Presidency Translator is a neural machine translation (NMT) system developed, among others, for the trio presidency in 2017 and 2018, i.e. the EU Council Presidencies of Estonia (translate2017.eu), Bulgaria and Austria (translate2018.eu).
For the Austrian Council Presidency in 2018, the system was geared towards texts related to the Presidency domains, thereby specializing in the language directions German-English and English-German. The neural machine translation system was targeted at EU Council Presidency staff, journalists, translators, delegates and visitors. For the Austrian Presidency, the objective was the creation of customized machine translation (MT) engines for the English and Austrian German language pair with a focus on domains and text types related to the work program of the EU Council Presidency.
For the training of the EU Council Presidency Translator for Austria, the following categories of data were collected and are available through the Portal:
1. Austria-related named entities (names of municipalities, names of politicians, common first names and last names of people, etc.) were collected and compiled from Open Data (common names and geographical names), Wikimedia (names of stock companies) and manually compiled (names of politicians, Austrian newspapers, etc.) (15,000 named entities).
The Austrian Open Data Portal (www.data.gv.at) proved to be a useful resource containing data such as named entities (municipalities, regions, common first and last names, etc.). Although the Austrian Open Data Portal listed a rather large amount of language resources, several of these language resources required further processing due to the file formats used, e.g. PDF.
2. German-English parallel data containing news and statements (press releases, interviews and Common Foreign and Security Policy statements) in German and English by the Presidency of the Council of the EU held by Austria in 2006, aligned with HunAlign, a language-independent sentence aligner (Varga et al, 2005) and

manually evaluated by two evaluators (4,973 translation units in .tmx format).
3. Austria-related named entities and terminology related to the topics of the trio presidency was created by the University of Vienna by crawling, extracting and compiling content from Wikipedia (71,000 terms, .txt format).
4. Additionally, a German-English terminological database of the core Austrian administrative terminology outlined in 3.1 was used for the purpose of MT training (1,400 terms).
When collecting these Austrian-German-specific LRs, the major obstacles were not the lack of relevant data, but the rather restrictive usage rights and legal uncertainties related to crawling, collecting, sharing and using the language data. For this reason, the following data are not part of the Portal, although collected and deemed useful for MT training and other NLP applications:
For the news domain covering Austria, two monolingual corpora were compiled. The Austrian German news corpus (2.3 M segments) was compiled from news gathered by focused crawling of all major Austrian daily broadsheets, and press releases from major news and media outlets produced in Austria. For the English news, several sub-corpora were compiled (2.3 M segments) by focused crawling of news and media platforms in Austria, in Germany and at the European level on the topic "Austria".
For the EU Council Presidency domain and its main topics, monolingual and parallel corpora were compiled. A monolingual Austrian German corpus was compiled by focused crawling of websites of relevant public entities. The corpus for training the EU Council Presidency Translator contained a large amount of texts produced in Austria. This is in contrast to eTranslation, the European Commission's machine translation system (for German), which is mainly trained with LRs from Germany. This is also illustrated by the large amount of LRs provided by Germany in ELRC-SHARE (elrc-share.eu/repository), which makes accessible openly licensed LRs that are used for the training of the eTranslation engines.
Our data collection efforts showed that there is a certain number of language resources, which are available to be implemented in language technology applications available for the Austrian German variety in the public administration domain. These resources had to be pre-processed in order to make them suitable for further use.

3.2 Language Guide

The Austrian Language Resource Portal also offers a language guide that provides basic information on communication in English. It contains tips, e.g. for having small talk, chairing a meeting, writing an e-mail, ordering food in the restaurant, explaining culinary specialties or identifying false friends. Moreover, it provides information on avoiding pitfalls in intercultural communication. It is targeted at people who are not used to speak English. It proved to be a useful aid in language learning contexts.

3.3 Compilation of other Language Resources

Finally, the Austrian Language Resource Portal contains a compilation of other relevant language resources and repositories that were not created by the cooperation partners as part of the Portal. Thus, links to external terminological databases that are especially relevant for translators and interpreters are provided.
An overview of all LRs on the Austrian Language Resource Portal is available on the website: sprachressourcen.at.

4. Discussion and Conclusion

The Austrian Language Resource Portal reflects the need for a central platform to access and exchange language resources that are specific to the Austrian variety of the German language. It provides a first attempt to not only highlight the value of language resources and make them freely available, but also show the impact of language resource sharing (Heinisch, 2018). Nevertheless, the amount of language resources on this Portal is not a comprehensive and exhaustive one. This may be due to the fact that the Austrian Language Resource Portal is primarily aimed at the target group of language professionals, such as translators. This is also the reason why the language resources are made available in different formats with giving preference to human-readable formats over machine-readable ones.
Additionally, major obstacles for delivering language resources to the Portal are confidentiality and security issues, legal uncertainty, i.e. the question of whether translators are allowed to share data due to IPR or copyright issues as well as the organizational framework that hinders the delivery of language resources. This shows that in Austria, similar to the situation all over Europe, there is still a lack of awareness for the value of language data (Heinisch and Kotzian, 2018; European Language Resource Coordination, 2019). Nevertheless, these language resources would be especially important for training human language technology, including machine translation systems, with a lower-resourced language variety to achieve quality improvements in language technology output.
The availability of and access to language resources in a language variety, such as Austrian German, may improve NLP and language technology applications (e.g. NMT training and thus increase the quality of NMT output), to avoid the deprivation of language diversity (within a language). This is particularly important in the light of the European Parliament resolution on language equality in the digital age, which recognizes that some (smaller) languages are threatened by digital extinction (EP, 2018). The resolution also states that language technologies can overcome language barriers and facilitate communication in a multilingual European Digital Single Market. Furthermore, the language equality resolution recommends that the member states of the EU define a minimum number of language resources for each European language to counteract digital extinction. These language resources may include lexicons, annotated corpora, speech records, translation memories and encyclopedic content (ibid.). The Austrian Language Resource Portal aims at contributing to this objective by increasing the availability of and access to language-variety-specific language resources.
In this respect, the Portal stresses the significance of differentiating between varieties of German and thus primarily caters for the Austrian German variety. This demonstrates that especially languages for specific purposes may differ significantly between the different standard varieties of the German language, as exemplified by the terminology used in public administration.
Although the Austrian Language Resource Portal focuses on Austrian German it does not mention other Austrian

language varieties, such as dialects, which play a crucial role in Austria. Thus, areas such as non-standard language, e.g. dialects (in machine translation) (Neubarth & Trost, 2017) would require further investigation.
To sum up, the Austrian Language Resource Portal stresses the importance of language resources specific to a language variety, thus paving the way for the re-use of variety-specific language data for human language technology, such as MT training, for the Austrian standard variety.

5. Acknowledgements

This work has been partly funded by the European Union's Connecting Europe Facility under grant agreement no. INEA/CEF/ICT/A2016/1297953. We would also like to thank Jürgen Kotzian from the Austrian Armed Forces Language Institute, who was spearheading the creation of the Austrian Language Resource Portal and Bartholomäus Wloka from the Centre for Translation Studies for his support in LR collection.

6. Bibliographical References

Clyne, M. G. (1995). The German language in a changing Europe. Cambridge: Cambridge University Press.

de Cilia, R. and Wodak, R. (2002). Zwischen Monolingualität und Mehrsprachigkeit. Zur Geschichte der österreichischen Sprachenpolitik. In H. Barkowski & R. Faistauer (Eds.), *in Sachen Deutsch als Fremdsprache. Sprachenpolitik und Mehrsprachigkeit, Unterricht, Interkulturelle Begegnung*. Hohengehren: Schneider Verlag, pp. 12-27.

de Groot, G.-R. (1999). Zweisprachige juristische Wörterbücher. In P. Sandrini (Ed.), *Übersetzen von Rechtstexten. Fachkommunikation im Spannungsfeld zwischen Rechtsordnung und Sprache*. Tübingen: Narr, pp. 203–227.

DIN ISO 18587:2018-02 Übersetzungsdienstleistungen_-Posteditieren maschinell erstellter Übersetzungen - Anforderungen. Berlin: Beuth Verlag GmbH.

European Language Resource Coordination (2019). ELRC White Paper. Sustainable Language Data Sharing to Support Language Equality in Multilingual Europe. Why Language Data Matters. http://www.lr-coordination.eu/sites/default/files/ELRC_Conference/ELRCWhitePaper.pdf.

EP (2018). European Parliament resolution of 11 September 2018 on language equality in the digital age. http://www.europarl.europa.eu/doceo/document/TA-8-2018-0332_EN.html.

Heinisch, B. (2018). Dissemination of administrative terminology on Austria's language resource portal as a means of quality assurance. Poster presentation at the EAFT Terminology Summit 2019, San Sebastian, Spain.

Heinisch, B. (2020). Sprachvarietätenabhängige Terminologie in der neuronalen maschinellen Übersetzung: Eine Analyse in der Sprachrichtung Englisch-Deutsch mit Schwerpunkt auf der österreichischen Varietät der deutschen Sprache. In C. Schöch (Ed.), DHd 2020 Spielräume: *Digital Humanities zwischen Modellierung und Interpretation. Konferenzabstracts*, pp. 211–214.

Heinisch, B. and Kotzian, J. (2018). ELRC Workshop Report for Austria: Deliverable D3.2.10. http://lr-coordination.eu/sites/default/files/Austria/2018/ELRC_Workshop_Austria_Report_public_v1_FINAL.PDF.

Lohaus, M. (2000). Recht und Sprache in Österreich und Deutschland: Gemeinsamkeiten und Verschiedenheiten als Folge geschichtlicher Entwicklungen; Untersuchung zur juristischen Fachterminologie in Österreich und Deutschland. Giessen, Fachverl. Köhler.

Markhardt, H. (2002). Das österreichische Deutsch im Rahmen der Europäischen Union : das "Protokoll Nr. 10 über die Verwendung österreichischer Ausdrücke der deutschen Sprache" zum österreichischen EU-Beitrittsvertrag und die Folgen: eine empirische Studie zum österreichischen Deutsch in der EU, Univ. Wien.

Neubarth, F. and Trost, H. (2017). Statistische maschinelle Übersetzung vom Standarddeutschen in den Wiener Dialekt. In C. Resch & W.U. Dressler (Eds.), *Digitale Methoden der Korpusforschung*. Wien, Verlag der österreichischen Akademie der Wissenschaften, pp. 179–203.

Schmidlin, R. (2011). Die Vielfalt des Deutschen: Standard und Variation: Gebrauch, Einschätzung und Kodifizierung einer plurizentrischen Sprache. Studia linguistica Germanica. Berlin: De Gruyter.

Schreiber, M. (2002). Austriazismen in der EU: (k)ein Übersetzungsproblem? *Lebende Sprachen*, 47(4). https://doi.org/10.1515/les.2002.47.4.150

Varga Dániel, Péter Halácsy, András Kornai, Viktor Nagy, László Németh & Viktor Trón (2005). Parallel corpora for medium density languages. Proceedings of RANLP'2005. Borovets, Bulgaria, pp. 590-596.

Wiesinger, P. (1996). Das österreichische Deutsch als eine Varietät der deutschen Sprache. *Die Unterrichtspraxis / Teaching German*, 29, 1996: 10.2307/3531825.

Wiesinger, P., Ed. (1988). Das österreichische Deutsch. Wien, Köln, Graz, Böhlau.

Wissik, T. (2013). Terminologische Variation in der Rechts- und Verwaltungssprache: eine korpusbasierte Analyse der Hochschulterminologie in den Standardvarietäten des Deutschen in Deutschland, Österreich und der Schweiz. Dissertation, Universität Wien.

7. Language Resource References

ARG GUT (2018). Fachglossar Österreichische Verwaltung. Deutsch – Englisch, distributed via Sprachressourcenportal Österreichs, https://www.sprachressourcen.at/verwaltungsglossar/

University of Vienna (2018). Austrian named entities, distributed via ELRC-SHARE, https://www.elrc-share.eu/repository/browse/austrian-named-entities/b0998b12ab9611e8b7d400155d02670612bad73492934202887a45e227312e0e/

University of Vienna (2018). Glossary terms in German related to Austria and the topics of the trio presidency, distributed via ELRC-SHARE, https://www.elrc-share.eu/repository/browse/terms-in-german-related-to-austria-and-the-topics-of-the-trio-presidency/b82781c4ab9e11e8b7d400155d026706f61ef02809fb4748944b1af1b434f0a9/

University of Vienna (2018). German-English parallel data by the Presidency of the Council of the EU held by Austria in 2006, distributed via ELRC-SHARE, https://www.elrc-share.eu/repository/browse/german-english-parallel-data-by-the-presidency-of-the-council-of-the-eu-held-by-austria-in-2006/e38b283eac3e11e8b7d400155d0267062180d233a0fd4e84b8dffb9b25cc1775/

Proceedings of the First workshop on Language Technologies for Government and Public Administration (LT4Gov), pages 32–36
Language Resources and Evaluation Conference (LREC 2020), Marseille, 11–16 May 2020
© European Language Resources Association (ELRA), licensed under CC-BY-NC

Legal-ES: A Set of Large Scale Resources for Spanish Legal Text Processing

Doaa Samy°*, Jerónimo Arenas-García, David Pérez-Fernández
Instituto de Ingeniería del Conocimiento & Cairo University*,
Universidad Carlos III de Madrid,
Ministerio de Economía (Secretaría de Estado para la Digitalización e Inteligencia Artificial)
°IIC, C/Tomás Francisco y Valiente, Campus Universitario, Cantoblanco, Madrid, Spain
*Cairo University, Main Campus, Giza 12613, Egypt
Universidad Carlos III de Madrid, Leganés, Madrid, Spain
Secretaría de Estado para la Digitalización e Inteligencia Artificial, C/Poeta Joan Maragall 41, Madrid, Spain
doaa.samy@iic.uam.es & doaasamy@cu.edu.eg, jarenas@ing.uc3m.es, dperezf@mineco.es

Abstract

This paper presents work on progress aiming at the development of Legal-ES. Legal-ES is a set of resources for Spanish legal text processing including a large scale corpus with calculated models for word embeddings and topics. The large scale Spanish legal corpus consists of over 2000 million words from open public legislative, jurisprudential and administrative texts representing a variety of sources from international, national and regional entities. The corpus is pre-processed and tokenized. A word embedding is calculated over raw text and over lemmatised texts in addition to some experiments with topic modelling on the legislative subset of the corpus representing the text from the Spanish Official Bulletin of State (Boletin Oficial del Estado-BOE). Within the framework of the Workshop on Language Technologies for Government and Public Administration (LT4Gov), the present paper showcases how Public Data is a valuable input for developing Language Resources. It fits within the second dimension of the workshop, i.e. PublicData4LRs. Legal-ES is the result of an initiative by the team of the Spanish Plan for the Advancement of Language Technologies (Plan TL) aiming at developing resources for the HLT community to promote intelligent solutions by industry and academia destined to Public Administration and the Legal Domain.

Keywords: Language Resources, Legal Corpus, Embeddings, Topic Modelling, Legislative text, Spanish Resources

1. Introduction

In the legal domain, Human Language Technologies (HLT) and Natural Language Processing (NLP) have been gaining more and more attention over the last years. HLT and NLP are marking a significant difference in handling the large sets of documents and data usually managed by stakeholders in the legal domain, especially when applied in Information Retrieval and Information Extraction.

Within the Spanish National Plan for the Advancement of Language Technologies (Plan TL), priority domains are selected to develop pilot projects. The Legal domain has been one of these priority areas in the last two years given its relevance and its impact on society at the different levels: Governmental bodies' level, industry, academia, services for citizens, structural measures, etc. Conversations were held at different levels with Public and Regional Administrations as well as academic and industrial groups to gain first-hand insights on the current situation of NLP applied in the Legal domain within the context of the Spanish language and co-official languages (Catalan, Basque and Galician).

From the perspective of the National Spanish Plan, the Public Administration would play a relevant role in promoting the NLP industry in the legal domain by adopting NLP-based solutions in real case scenarios and by providing more legal public datasets to allow for developing innovative and intelligent components. These components would contribute to the Digital Transformation of Public Administration and would introduce innovative workflows turning traditional procedures into more effective and less-time-consuming tasks towards better services to the citizens. At the European level, initiatives such as e-Codex or e-Justice aiming at improving legal services for EU citizens by facilitating the exchange of legal information, are examples of the opportunities and the needs within this domain.

On the other hand, Spanish language is one of the top widely spoken languages, but most of the language resources developed for the legal domain are mainly in English. So, there is a justified need to develop resources in Spanish.

Development of Corpora of legal texts started some years ago. Vogel et al. (2017) lists some of the available corpora. BLaRC (The British Law Report Corpus) is an example of these efforts. The British English corpus is made up of judicial decisions and issued by British courts and tribunals consisting of 8.5 million words published between 2008 and 2010. The American Law Corpus (ALC) consists of 5.5 million words, while the Corpus of European Law includes a billion word in English and German.

Recent work concerning resources has focused on compiling large datasets and on applying deep learning techniques to train word2vec models. Chalkidis & Kampas (2019) shared word embeddings trained over a large dataset of legislations from UK, EU, Canada, Australia, USA and Japan among others. Nay (2016) published "Gov2vec" in which policies are compared across institutions by embedding representations of the legal corpus of each institution and the vocabulary shared across all corpora into a continuous vector space. The corpus used included 59 years of all U.S. Supreme Court opinions, 227 years of all U.S. Presidential Actions and 42 years of official summaries of all bills introduced in the U.S. Congress. Sugathadasa et al. (2017) used word2vec and lexicons for semantic similarity in the legal domain. Embeddings were calculated over a corpus of 35000 legal case documents, pertaining to various areas of practices in law from US Supreme Court.

Other examples of related work in the legal domain regarding specific applications or aspects of legal text processing include, among other, predictive models for decision support in administrative adjudication (Branting et al. 2017), contract element extraction (Chalkidis, 2017), legal question answering (Do, 2017) (Kim, 2015),

extracting requisite and effectuation parts in legal texts (Nguyen et al., 2018) and classification of sentential modalities (O'Neill et al, 2017).
State of art reveals the increasing interest, the variety of applications and the vast opportunities for HLT and NLP in the legal domain. Nevertheless, the dominance of the English language in most of the resources and the work done is obvious and there is a clear need for resources in other languages including Spanish, especially given that the industrial uptake would have an international wide impact on Spanish speaking countries.

2. Legal-ES: The Corpus

Legal-ES is a large scale Spanish corpus of over 2000 million words representing different types of legislative, administrative and jurisprudential texts. All datasets are gathered from open public portals, mainly from Spain, Europe and International organizations in addition to resources from Mexican and Argentinian portals. For the harvesting, we opted for the availability and the openness of the resource rather than balanced representations in certain time frames.

Figure 1. Resources for Legal-ES

Legal-ES is designed in six consecutive phases to allow for a wider coverage and access. Phases are applied on the different subsets according to the characteristics of each dataset with different timeframes:

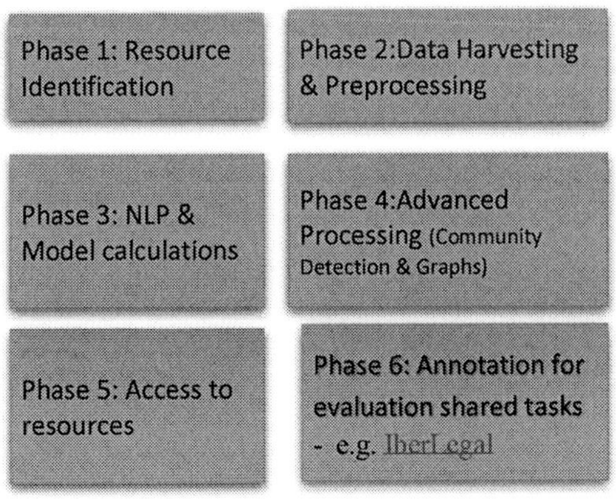

At Phase 1, a number of sources were identified. Also, the legal aspects of some resources are subject of study and analysis by legal experts within the team. Nevertheless, a regular update is needed to add newly identified resources and to update the already available ones given the dynamic nature as legislations, sentences, public procurement etc. are in a continuous increase. Resources are identified in **four sets** according to the type. Table 1 summarizes ***Set 1 the preliminary list*** including: Legislations from the Official Bulletin (BOE), Opinions from State Council, Consultations from State Tax Agency, State Advocacy, Fiscal Doctrine, the Spanish subset of the European EurLex and JRC-Acquis dataset.

Name	Number of words
Legislación BOE	547.615.892
Doctrina Fiscalía	2.684.855
Dictámenes Consejo de Estado	135.348.664
Abogacía del Estado	6.123.007
Códigos electrónicos	24.261.786
Consultas tributarias	401.586.826
JRC-Acquis	59.155.891
EurLex	58.005.420

Table 1. Set 1: Identified Datasets and Size

Set 2: Additional legislative resources (238 million words) including:

- Legislations from Mexico Data Portal
- Legislations from Argentina Data Portal

Set 3: Additional jurisprudential resources including:

- Open public sentences from Spanish Supreme Court
- Open public sentences involving Spanish regional authorities (Madrid & Barcelona among others)
- Open public sentences from regional courts in Mexico
- Resolutions from the International Court of Justice (Spanish versions)

Set 4: Further administrative resources including:
- Public Procurement from the Spanish Platform
- Spanish versions of Public Procurement posted on EU Tender Daily Platform.
- Public Procurement from the Mexican Public Procurement Platform.

A selection of resources from the different sets have passed the legal check to ensure compliance to the open data licenses and thus proceeded to Phase 2, i.e. they are already harvested and pre-processed. This selection includes: All legislative sources in Set 1, the jurisprudential texts from the Supreme Court (Set 3) and the administrative texts from Spanish Public Procurement (Set 4). We will refer to this subset as Legal-ES/IberLegal.

3. Word Embeddings and Topic Modelling

For Phase 3: NLP & Model Calculations, two experiments for Word Embeddings were conducted. The first over the raw text in Set 1 and the second over the lemmatised subset of BOE legislations in ***Set 1***. Embeddings were trained over 300 dimensions and were collapsed to 2 dimensions for representation purposes as in Figure 3 at the end of this setcion. Both experiments showed interesting results. In figure 3, the square on the left shows a cluster with varieties of wine, while the square on the upper right shows words related to posts with near embeddings. The right square down shows words related to taxes.

Moreover, we tested introducing some words in different semantic fields to check the words with the nearest embeddings. For example, by introducing the words "impuesto [tax]", we found the nearest embeddings "renta [income]", "tributo [tribute]", etc. Also, by checking the word "ley [law]", the nearest embeddings were "orden_ministerial [ministerial_order]", "decreto [decree]", "decreto_real [royal_decree]", etc. In the agricultural domain, when the word "wine [vino]" was introduced, the nearest embeddings were types of wine such as "chardonnay", "merlot", "pinot", etc.

```
Legislations
-'orden_ministerial' [Ministerial-order],
(0.8387089967727661),
-'reales_decretos'[Royal_Decree],
(0.8019422888755798),
-'decreto'[Decree],(0.7804737091064453),
-'real_decreto-ley' [Royal_Decree_Law],
(0.7155911326408386),
-'orden' [Order], (0.6945813894271851),
- 'ley'[Law], (0.6891162991523743)
```

```
Taxes
[-('irpf.', 0.7073756456375122),
 -('i.r.p.f.', 0.5817404389381409),
 -('impuesto'[Tax], 0.5020797848701477),
 -('renta'[Income],
0.46861714124679565),
 -('tributo' [tribute],
0.46004000306129456),
 -('impuestos[tax]',
0.45298290252685547),
('impuesto_de_sociedades'[Societies´tax]
, 0.444973886013031),
]
```

Regarding the Topic Modelling, different models (25, 40, 50 and 150) were trained over the subset of BOE legislations. Trained models of 25 and 40 showed good results with clear topics identified as shown in the examples in Table 2 and Figure 4. Table 2 represents an extract from the topic model-25 with the most representative words for the selected topics. In Figure 4, an example of topic representation in a document where there is a clear dominance of the topic 13 related to "Fishing legislations". This would also contribute in identifying semantic similarities among documents based on topic representation.

Topic	Word	Word	Word
Education & Universities	universitario	educación [education]	enseñanza [teaching]
Taxes	ayuda [aid]	gasto [expenditure]	pago [payment]
Workers	trabajo [work]	empresa [company]	convenio [agreement]
Agreements & Cooperation	partes [parts]	protocolo [protocol]	país [country]

Table 2. Example of Topics (Model-25)

In Phase 4- Advanced Processing, further experimentations were carried out to detect communities of similar documents, however results are still at very preliminary stage that needs further analysis. An example of the graph representations of the communities is the following. Nodes are documents and edges link documents with high semantic similarities:

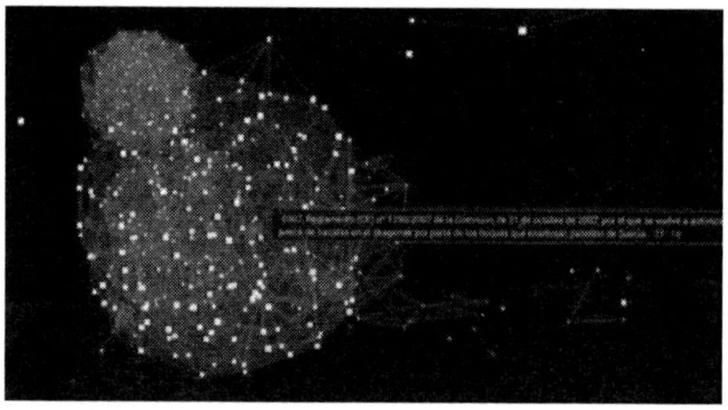

Figure 5. Community Detection in BOE

Finally, at Phase 5, access to the code that facilitates the downloading of the open public resources of BOE was made available on Github.

4. Future Steps: Annotation and Evaluation Shared Tasks

Currently, the process of annotation of Named Entities has started in samples from Legal-ES/IberLegal. The annotation is carried out via bootstrapping, i.e. initial manual annotation is fed into automatic annotation through an iterative method with a final manual validation and an inter-annotator agreement to obtain a gold standard set. The annotation considers five types of Named Entities:

- Persons - Institutions
- Time expressions -Locations
- References to laws and legislations.

Sample fragments from legislations, sentences and public procurement are annotated over Brat Platform.

The annotation is still at an exploratory stage, but it is quite challenging specially that the distribution of the Named

Entities and the complexity of the annotation varies among the different types of texts. For example, legislations from BOE follow a normalised style making the annotation easier, while administrative texts of public procurement are much more cumbersome given the broad diversity of the procurement texts and the lack of normalised forms.
The annotated set will be made available within an evaluation shared tasks named after the sample corpus "IberLegal". The task is organised within the Spanish Evaluation Campaign "Iberlef". For the annotation, experiments were carried out for Named Entities annotation using open libraries such as Spacy, FreeLing or IXA Pipes, however, the generic tools performed poorly on this type of texts, specially in detecting references of laws. This revealed a clear need for Named Entity Recognition and Classification components adapted to the legal domain in Spanish. Based on these findings, the team at the Spanish Language Technologies Plan decided to organise IberLegal as the first shared task focusing on Named Entities Recognition in Spanish legal and administrative text.

5. Conclusion

In this paper, we presented a showcase of Public Data as Language Resources where we introduced the ongoing work to develop Legal-ES as a large scale language resource for Spanish legal text processing. The paper outlined the development phases and the progress achieved to date. Through this showcase, we share a possible roadmap of how to start from an open public data resource until reaching to a mature language resource and how to engage the community in the development of measurable components and advances. The actions taken are just steps on the way, but more work and effort is needed to achieve a solid infrastructure that allows for further developments

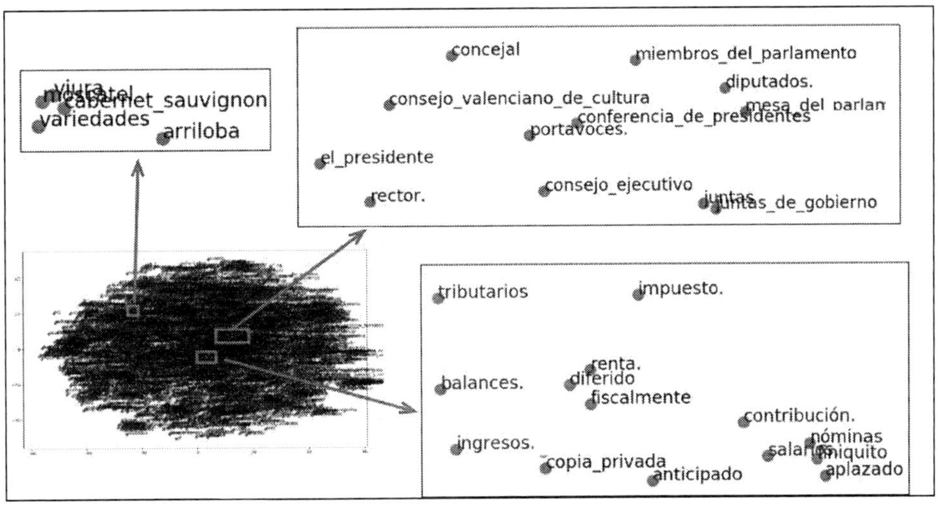

Figure 3. Representations of Word Embeddings-Set 1

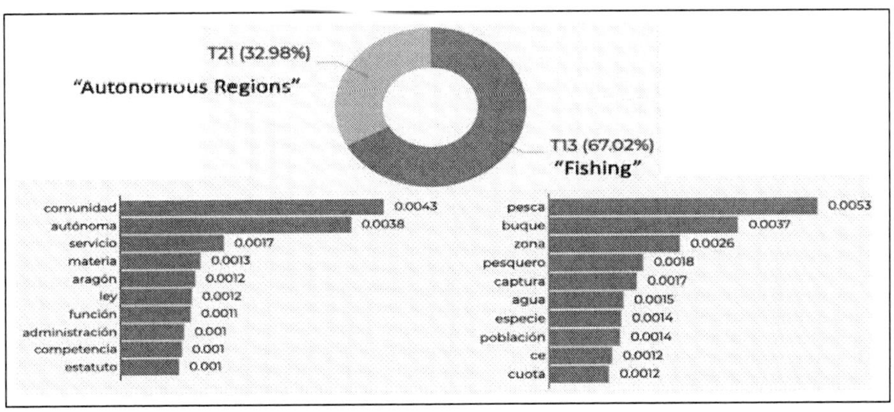

Figure 4. Document Representation through Topics

6. Bibliographical References

Branting LK, Yeh A, Weiss B, Merkhofer E, Brown B (2017). Inducing predictive models for decision support in administrative adjudication. In: Proceedings of the MIREL Workshop on the The 16th International Conference on Artificial Intelligence and Law, London, UK.

Chalkidis I, Androutsopoulos I (2017) A deep learning approach to contract element extraction. In: Proceedings of the 30th International Conference on Legal Knowledge and Information Systems, Luxembourg, pp 155–164.

Chalkidis, I., Kampas, D. (2019). Deep learning in law: early adaptation and legal word embeddings trained on large corpora. Artif Intell Law 27, 171–198 (2019). https://doi.org/10.1007/s10506-018-9238-9.

Do PK, Nguyen HT, Tran CX, Nguyen MT, Nguyen ML (2017). Legal Question Answering using Ranking SVM and Deep Convolutional Neural Network. CoRR abs/1703.0. arXiv:1703.05320.

O'Neill J, Buitelaar P, Robin C, Brien LO (2017). Classifying Sentential Modality in Legal Language: A Use Case in Financial Regulations, Acts and Directives. In: Proceedings of the 16th international conference on artificial intelligence and law, London, UK, pp 159–168.

Nay JJ (2016) Gov2vec: Learning distributed representations of institutions and their legal text. In: Proceedings of the first workshop on NLP and computational social science. Association for Computational Linguistics, pp 49–54, Austin, Texas. DOI:10.18653/v1/W16-5607

Nguyen T, Nguyen L, Tojo S, Satoh K, Shimazu A (2018). Recurrent neural network-based models for recognizing requisite and effectuation parts in legal texts. Artif Intell Law 26(2):169–199

Kim My, Xu Y, Goebel R (2015) A convolutional neural network in legal question answering. In: Ninth International Workshop on Juris-informatics (JURISIN).

Sugathadasa, K., Ayesha, B., Silva, N.D., Perera, A., Jayawardana, V., Lakmal, D., & Perera, M. (2017). Synergistic union of Word2Vec and lexicon for domain specific semantic similarity. 2017 IEEE International Conference on Industrial and Information Systems (ICIIS), 1-6. DOI:10.1109/ICIINFS.2017.8300343.

Vogel, F., Hammann, H. and Gauer, I (2017). Computer-Assisted Legal Linguistics: Corpus Analysis as a New Tool for Legal Studies. Law & Social Inquiry, 2017. DOI: https://doi.org/10.1111/lsi.12305.

Association for Computational Linguistics
209 N. Eighth Street
Stroudsburg, Pennsylvania 18360

ISBN 978-1-7138-1268-5

CURRAN ASSOCIATES INC.
proceedings.com